The **IDEA** Mindset

'A must-read for people who know something needs to change but don't know where to start. Conquer your FOMO and get a copy of *The IDEA Mindset*'

PATRICK MCGINNIS, INVENTOR OF FOMO,
HOST OF FOMO SAPIENS PODCAST, AUTHOR

'Gary intuitively connects you with the power of your natural talents and strengths to help you design your perfect future working life'

DANA WILLIAMS, CREATOR OF THE STRENGTHS JOURNAL™
AND FORMER SENIOR MARKETING LEADER AT SOUTHWEST
AIRLINES

'I can't understate how transformative this IDEA programme has been for me. I really like how this programme emphasises how I can use my unique strengths to develop my own unique leadership style'

CRAIG STRONG, GLOBAL PRODUCT & INNOVATION
PRACTICE LEAD, AMAZON WEB SERVICES (AWS)

'The IDEA philosophy helped me reconnect with my inner voice and enlighten my career path and relationships using my unique talents'

MARIETTA MELROSE, ACTRESS AND PRODUCER

THE

DR GARY CROTAZ PhD

IDEA
MINDSET

FIGURE OUT WHAT YOU WANT FROM WORK AND HOW TO GET IT, IN 6 WEEKS

First published in 2022 by Dr Gary Crotaz, PhD
In partnership with whitefox publishing

www.garycrotaz.com

Paperback ISBN 978-1-913532-90-1
eBook ISBN 978-1-913532-91-8

Edited by Rachel Kenny
Designed and typeset by Couper Street Type Co.
Printed and bound by TJ Books

For Mildred, Mochi and Beansprout – three hearts
and eight paws that inspire me every day.

For my parents, who have always supported me
in figuring out my own path, however winding.

With grateful thanks to my editor Rachel Kenny, John Bond, Julia
Koppitz, Chris Wold and all the team at whitefox, Holly Kyte, Jess
Htay, Rebecca Gray, Dan Prescott and the team at Couper Street
Type Co., the fabulous creative team that is Cinta Miller, Alexis
Knox, also Adam Toomey and Lua Lema at Owl Studio Ltd.

Finally to Davide and Olga Cacciari and all at Team Diablo, and to
friends, colleagues and clients, past and present, who have inspired
me with your journeys of extraordinary change and self-discovery.

AUTHOR'S NOTE

Gallup CliftonStrengths® 34

Originally developed by the award-winning American psychologist Donald O. Clifton in 1999, CliftonStrengths 34 is a sophisticated scientific tool to help people understand and target their natural talents and strengths. Ninety per cent of Fortune 500 companies have used it, and over 25 million people around the world have now completed the CliftonStrengths assessment.

The power of CliftonStrengths goes far beyond the scope of this book – large organisations use it to help individuals and teams to perform at their best. All my private coaching clients complete the assessment as part of their coaching journey.

In Week 1 of the IDEA Mindset programme you are invited to complete the CliftonStrengths assessment and reflect on your personalised strengths profile. You purchase the assessment directly from the Gallup website. At the time of writing (2021) the cost of CliftonStrengths 34 is £50. The lower-cost CliftonStrengths Top 5 is £20.[1] The price varies in other markets. I do not receive any form of commission from Gallup if you purchase the assessment.

I believe that the best way to discover your strengths is with the CliftonStrengths assessment. However, you don't have to complete CliftonStrengths to get full value from *The IDEA Mindset*. An alternative approach to discovering your strengths is also provided in Week 1 to enable you to complete the exercises.

CONTENTS

INTRODUCTION:

What is the IDEA Mindset and what does it have to do with your career goals?

The IDEA Mindset is a way of thinking that will lead you towards a deeply fulfilling working life, based around the four core principles of **Identity**, **Direction**, **Engagement** and **Authenticity**. I've been developing the foundations of a programme that helps people access this mindset for almost 20 years. People who are unhappy in their jobs, people who have lost their sense of purpose, people who are striving for ambitious goals or are just wondering what to do next. People just like you.

Over the next six fun, intensive weeks, you will gain a profound understanding of your natural strengths. You will design a working life that enables you to reach your fullest potential, that excites you every day and delivers on what *you* need from your work – emotionally, logistically and everything in between – and you'll draw up a clear and comprehensive plan for how to get there. Finally, and most importantly, you will access the confidence, clarity and calm that comes with knowing where you're going, and why: your IDEA Mindset.

This is your chance to change your life. Grasp it with both hands!

My Story: From Medicine, to Corporate Strategy, to Ballroom Dancing

I've been coaching and mentoring people who are navigating changes in their working lives ever since I stepped away from a career as a doctor almost 20 years ago. I'd spent eight years studying the sciences, training on the hospital wards, teaching anatomy and undertaking medical research in Bristol and Cambridge. In the months leading up to my final exams, I realised I was on completely the wrong path for me. Facing a crisis of identity, I pulled the escape cord and threw myself into the unknown in the business world, breaking convention and leaving behind so much that I had built up over the years. But for all that I lost, I found even more – new career choices that played to my true strengths, exciting opportunities, a sense of drive and purpose.

In those early years after leaving medicine, I did a lot of mentoring for medics going through that same experience of questioning their choices. It was always sobering to see others going through a similar career crisis to the one I'd experienced. In helping others to find and shape their path, I started to discover my own passion for helping people achieve personal growth and change.

Post-medicine, alongside being a career coach and mentor, I also spent nearly a decade as a strategy consultant, helping businesses plan for the future. I helped clients understand their purpose and values, create vision statements, set strategic goals, define action plans and tell their story. Along the way, I would regularly spend time with colleagues, helping them to work out their future career choices and talking about similar 'strategic' questions: *where are you now? Where do you want to go? How are you going to get there? What do you need to do right now?* This period of my career helped crystallise the value of a clear sense of **Identity** and **Direction** – the first tenets of the IDEA Mindset.

With the free time I had left outside of the day job and the coaching, I was doing amateur ballroom dancing competitions with Mildred, a dance partner I'd met through work. I'd always loved to dance ever since I was very young, but the medical training had left no time for it, so I'd put it on the back burner. But meeting Mildred reignited my passion for dance and we were dedicating most of our evenings and weekends to practising and attending national competitions. At the start we improved very quickly, but as we came to the end of the fourth year of our partnership, we arrived at the demoralising realisation that our progress had plateaued. In January 2010, we arrived home from the UK Open Amateur Ballroom Championship, deeply depressed after another poor result. Over the previous few months we had been training hard in the studio and travelling every weekend to take dancing lessons with the top coaches. They had praised our effort and applauded our progress. But on the day, it was not enough, and the judges determined that we were not worthy of a place in the next round.

We looked back over the last four years of our partnership, the huge amount of effort, time and money expended, and felt we hadn't achieved our potential. We knew we had a good few headwinds against us, but we were highly motivated and passionate about becoming the best we could possibly be. We were older than most of our competitors, that was certainly true, and having to hold down full-time jobs to earn the money to train and compete put us at a disadvantage compared with couples who had funding or sponsorship. We had made the top 24 couples in the British Championship three years in a row, but now we wanted to progress and break through to the next level. We felt as though we were stagnating, and we knew that at our age we were running out of time.

We sat down together that night and had a heart-to-heart.

We loved to dance. We loved training and learning. We loved the challenge. We were both highly competitive. We had made many friends from around the world.

We also hated losing. We hated the feeling of being in a rut. We hated that when we tried with every ounce of our being the results didn't come. We hated not being in control.

We were spending six nights a week in the studio, funnelling all our passion and every spare penny into the pursuit of our dream. We hadn't taken a proper holiday in years. Our careers outside of dance were compromised because of the time commitment.

Over the years, we had pulled all the levers to try to step up to the next level. We had got fitter, changed our choreography, changed our look, changed our coaches, changed our training regime. We had left good jobs to have more time to train. Yet despite all that, it hadn't brought us the success and fulfilment we were searching for.

This time we knew we were done. Not with dancing overall, but with *this* dancing. *This* approach, *this* strategy, *this* plan.

Neither of us were ready to retire, but this equation didn't add up. The sacrifices did not justify the rewards. We were passionate about our goals, but we weren't foolish. We knew this wasn't the way.

We knew there was one alternative. One we'd ruled out for years because it was too crazy an idea, too ridiculous a thought. But now we were in the territory of crazy ideas.

We'd heard about Team Diablo a year or two before – an elite training club in Italy where top couples congregate from around the world. Virtually none were from the UK.

In our studio you hardly heard it mentioned, even though it was the training hub of the world champions at the time. There was virtually no information available on the internet; everything was by word of mouth. But then we also knew of some of the couples from the school and we trusted what we could see with our own eyes.

What had stopped us going before were the practicalities. We were based in London; they were based just outside Bologna, Italy. Our jobs were busy – often 50-plus hours per week – and based in central London or around the UK. They trained every day, Monday to Friday, and travelled around Europe every weekend to compete. We didn't have the money to be able to quit work completely. Nothing made it seem in any way feasible.

But now the question in front of us was starker than ever: should we retire gracefully to a life of comfort and relaxation or go bold and radical? We'd never particularly thought of ourselves as bold before. But we felt bold now. Mildred picked up the phone and spoke to Davide Cacciari,

Principal of Team Diablo. He had no idea who we were but said simply, 'Come visit.'

Opening Our Eyes to a New Mindset at Team Diablo

Davide met us on the first day in his school – a collection of industrial units in a tiny village an hour north of Bologna. He congratulated us for showing up. 'The most difficult step for any competitive ballroom couple to take is to walk through the doors of my school. Because you are here, I already know that you are committed to making a change.' I've always been an advocate of following your heart and jumping in with both feet, however crazy it seems. As US political icon, and first Black woman elected to Congress, Shirley Chisholm put it, 'You don't make progress by standing on the sidelines.'

Over the next few weeks and months we travelled to Italy at every possible opportunity; two days here, two days there – whenever we could fit it in around work. We agreed with our bosses that we could split our holiday allocation into individual blocks of one or two days and that we would always take our laptops with us so we could work remotely if necessary. With no allocation left, we gave up on the idea of normal summer holidays, even a normal honeymoon when we got married. Ours was 24 hours in Venice followed by a week in a dance training camp!

We quickly realised how far off the mark we had been when looking at what we needed to do from our comfortable life in the UK. We became experts at booking the lowest cost of all low-cost flights, travelling at unsociable hours, flying to second-tier airports, getting the bus instead of a train or taxi, staying in the cheapest hotels – anything we could do to minimise the costs. We were teetering on the edge of feasibility, but we made it work. When we got to the studio, we were all in. Whatever we needed to do, we did.

The school had an Italian and Russian influence, driven by the Italian Davide and his Russian wife Olga. The Italian influence was all about elegance, artistry, athleticism and competition. The Russian approach was about discipline, rigour, excellence and unwavering commitment.

Here, life was difficult. Students arrived at the studio at eight in the morning and left at midnight. Training consisted of private lessons, group teaching and a lot of individual practice. Daily fitness and stamina training, nutrition and technical lectures filled the schedule. Every evening the school simulated the intensity of a competition, playing the music loud, bringing the lights down and creating the atmosphere of a live audience. Couples received individual feedback on their performance from qualified competition judges. Lectures were translated live from Italian into English for the benefit of the international dancers in the room. Dancers like us who visited from time to time were immersed in the same intensive training programme. Davide's rule was that every dancer had to participate in every aspect of the programme, no matter their education level or how many world championships they had won.

Outside the school there was nothing to do – just the village and then flat fields as far as the eye could see. Complete focus, no distractions. The local shopkeepers learned to recognise the familiar graceful physique and poise of the dancers. *'Ballerini, ballerini! – dancers, dancers!'* they exclaimed when we walked into the coffee shop for our therapeutic lunchtime espressos. We regularly met fellow students from as far afield as Vancouver and Vladivostok who were doing the same as us: attending the school every month.

Every weekend couples would get in a rickety minibus and drive through the night from Italy to a major competition somewhere in Europe. We trusted their dancing more than their driving, so we preferred to find a cheap flight and arrive in one piece! The school's leading couples routinely filled the top spots in every competition, from national through to world championships. Collectively the club held dozens of world-championship trophies, all posted on a screen in the entrance hall to inspire the students.

The whole set-up was established to reward exceptional performance and motivate us all to step up to the next level.

Here was a small collective of exceptional dancers training together on an industrial estate in rural Italy, with top teachers, college lecturers and a wise pair of coaches leading the programme. They created a difficult-to-access culture of excellence, hidden from the outside world. Immersing ourselves in this world changed our outlook on our dancing career and our whole perspective on what it takes to achieve your goals. It was a revelation.

Our dancing improved massively, our fitness was transformed and our whole outlook on training and competing was turned on its head.

Breaking Down Our Limiting Beliefs and Building a New and Empowering Mindset

As we reflected back on our experience with Team Diablo, we noticed frequent examples of when Davide was reframing our thinking and giving us the tools we needed to take control of our journey.

We thought we were fit enough, but honestly we'd had no idea. In the UK we had been training to dance five dances in a row, sometimes six or seven, to prepare ourselves for the physical demands of a competition. In Italy we had to dance 30 or 40 without a break. The first time we did it, we could hardly move the next day! We participated in an exercise called *tortura* which required us to stand on our toes without our heels touching the floor for 20 minutes at a time, switching between one foot and the other. We danced with weights and resistance bands, to the fastest music, together and separately. When it came to the competitions, we were finally ready to compete on a level playing field, where previously we'd always been half a step off the pace. What we learned: be physically and mentally ready to do what you plan to do.

7

We had learned the English technique, largely unchanged for decades, but now we discovered a new, much more sophisticated and complex technique of dance that enabled the creation of the dynamic movements and shapes that characterised the top couples. Our choreography was completely redesigned to play to our strengths and minimise our weaknesses. 'Why show the judges something you're not so good at doing?' said Davide in heavily accented English. 'If there's only one step that you are any good at dancing, then you can dance that same step over and over again until you get good enough at another one!' He meant it. What we learned: you are at your best when you focus on your strengths. Sometimes people see your weaknesses only because you put them on display.

We were used to competing alone. We were a team of two – us against the world. We used to think that was powerful because we felt we controlled our choices. What we were missing was the insight on all the things we didn't know. Now, when we went to competitions, we were part of a much bigger team. The more experienced couples were assigned to support us and give us feedback, both on the day and then back in the studio in the following weeks. As we got to know the system, we realised that almost all the top couples were part of a club system like this. It was almost invisible and we'd never seen it before. What we learned: sometimes you might not realise you need a support network … until you have a support network.

We felt we were putting a lot of effort in just to participate. Then one Saturday evening in Prague, we spoke to one of the top Dutch couples, Jan-Willem and Kendra. We asked them when their flight had arrived. 'Oh, we can't afford to take flights,' Kendra explained. 'Jan-Willem is a welder and I am a student. We both finished our work on Friday evening in Amsterdam and then drove through the night to get here to Prague to compete today.'

We looked it up: a ten-hour drive across the whole of Germany. 'Well, at least you get to sleep tonight before you drive home!' we said encouragingly.

'Oh no,' said Jan-Willem, 'we are leaving tonight to drive overnight to Paris and compete tomorrow.'

'Really?' I said, checking the map and seeing another 12-hour drive. 'You'll be taking some time off next week to rest, though?'

'We can't afford to take time off!' said Kendra. 'We're back to work first thing on Monday morning.'

Another couple left the studio in the evening and spent the next few hours cleaning offices. They were world champions, in a sport where the cost of funding your career often outweighs your prize money by a hundred to one. What we learned: all those years while we told ourselves it was impossible to make it happen, others were finding a way.

We had danced for years trying to please our coaches and the competition judges. 'Your problem,' Davide intoned, 'is that you are afraid of what they think. And I can see that you are afraid. You worry that you may not get it right. But I can tell you something that will free your mind. You will never get it right. You will never be perfect. And you will never be world champions. But you can become very accomplished dancers. You just have to let go of worrying about what everyone else thinks. Think of this: there is no such thing as right and wrong; there is only what you choose to do. They can choose whether to like it or not.' What we learned: we were limiting ourselves by creating a need for validation from others, instead of forging our own path.

These were the factors we had been missing when we'd been trying to break through before. Preparation, commitment, self-assurance and confidence. We'd always had passion and a desire to achieve our goals. Now we had the tools and the mindset that would help us to achieve our maximum potential. It felt as though someone had opened a door to show us a new world. Over the coming years we became confident, assertive competitors and developed our own style and creative flair. Our colleagues in our day jobs noticed the difference, too, in our determination and our clarity of purpose.

Our progression in Italy led us to represent England in the World and European championships as amateurs. After two years we decided to turn professional and competed at a further five World and European championships in the Professional Division. We knew that this was the peak of our capability and that we were never going to be vying for the top spots, but as we marched proudly in the parade of athletes at the World Championship in Moscow, we realised we'd achieved the dream we'd always wanted. The sacrifices had been worth it. Where my career in strategy helped to shape my understanding of Identity and Direction, so this part of my career helped develop my thinking around **Engagement** and **Authenticity** – the other two tenets of the IDEA Mindset.

After Dance: The Birth of the IDEA Mindset

Eventually, age caught up with me. We had just come back from the 2013 World Show Dance Championship in Italy. I was 37 years old – ten years older than most of the competitors. I'd had two knee operations and had been putting off a third for a year. The training was hard and the recovery was getting harder. I had come to the end of the road, and I knew in my heart that it was time. Retirement was harder on Mildred, who, being younger, could have continued on for a few years. It was a tough time as we accepted it was over.

Still, when we looked back on our whole dance career, it was amazing to reflect on what it had become. What had started as a bit of a pipe dream had taken us around the world and to extraordinary heights that we could never have imagined ten years before when we first started dancing together. We carried with us deep friendships, a wealth of memories and a new, empowering mindset that we would go on to apply in our future careers back in the real world.

Nonetheless, I couldn't get away from the fact that a major life shift had just taken place, and I needed to reconcile myself to it. I needed to work on articulating my radically different future career path to myself – one that I was going to be as excited about pursuing as I had been with dance.

As I picked up a pen to start writing some goals, I reflected on what my personal anchor points were when I thought about the work I wanted to do.

> To make a difference – to one person or to many
> To have control of my own destiny
> To be genuinely good at what I did
> To be bold in seeking out new paths
> To coach and mentor
> To bring this thinking to a wider audience

These were the foundations I needed to build upon to arrive at the next phase of my career. Crucially, each anchor point tapped into at least one of the IDEA tenets of **Identity**, **Direction**, **Engagement** and **Authenticity**: understanding my **Identity** beyond dance, finding clarity on my **Direction** of travel, building a future career as **Engaging** as the one I had just left and still connecting with my values and core purpose – my **Authenticity**. While I'd had the core principles of the IDEA Mindset simmering in the back of my mind for several years before we went to Italy, it wasn't until I brought together my thinking from my parallel careers in the business and elite sporting worlds that I understood the huge potential to be tapped when these four elements are fiercely present in your life.

Yes, the future was a big blank piece of paper, but I felt no anxiety, no self-doubt. Unlike when I left medicine – a moment of major anxiety that felt like stepping into the unknown – I now had real clarity about what was important to me and where I was at my absolute best: a combination of strategy and leadership, together with career coaching and mentoring, in organisations where I felt I could make a difference. My earlier crisis of identity had been replaced with confidence and self-assurance that even if I didn't have all the answers today, I could trust in my ability to navigate the path ahead and reach my full potential. I was excited about the future, and it was for me to design it and make it a reality.

Over the following six years I shaped my career with intention, beginning with those foundation anchor points. I took on new leadership positions, directing strategy and transformation programmes in a large retail business. I managed teams differently from before, using the new high-performance way of thinking I'd gained from my time as a professional dancer. I found a new balance between support and challenge, stretching the team's objectives to reach goals they hadn't thought were possible and creating the environment within which they could succeed. I aimed to empower my team members to develop their skills and grow into more impactful roles.

My coaching also evolved to become more challenging. I worked with those people who reported into me and coaching clients to create a mind-set that they could use to explore the opportunities their rational brain was telling them were out of reach.

I also became more assured about what I was good at and how I should spend my time. I let go of the things I didn't enjoy doing. I turned down opportunities when they didn't fit with my vision and purpose. I started doing more things for free if I felt they made a difference to someone. Eventually I went back to school for the first time in over 15 years to become a formally accredited executive coach. And I wrote a book. But you know that last bit already!

During the years after my retirement as a dancer, I gradually came to inhabit what I describe here as the IDEA Mindset, and it's something I completely embody today. I don't have the next ten years mapped out and I certainly don't have all the answers, but I feel clear and calm, with an inner compass that I know will guide me to a successful future.

I condensed what I'd discovered to be the most impactful exercises, tools and techniques for bringing about positive change in both myself and my coaching clients into a structured course of reflective exercises: the IDEA Programme®, which I created in 2018. This programme would connect my future coaching clients with their IDEA Mindset and guide them to build a robust action plan for reaching their most satisfying working life.

The axis of the programme was **Identity** and **Direction** – a journey from understanding your current situation through to setting goals, creating an action plan, executing that action plan and then telling your story to help others engage with the changes you are making. Around that axis I wove activities to build **Engagement** and **Authenticity**, values and strengths, resilience, physical wellness and taking ownership.

I put the IDEA Programme into practice with my coachees. Not only did they see huge changes in their working lives once they'd put their plans in motion, they also reported experiencing a profound growth in confidence – a mindset shift – that impacted many aspects of their lives. They had a new sense of purpose in work and in life, they could let go of what was frustrating them, they felt more confident about their choices and less regret about decisions they'd made in the past. Having seen the impact of the IDEA Programme, I know this is a model that works. At the heart of it is a strong sense of intentionality and ownership. Your purpose. Your goal. Your future. Your career.

The US mindset coach Steve Maraboli captures it perfectly: 'This is my life…my story…my book. I will no longer let anyone else write it; nor will I apologise for the edits I make.'

I realised that the power of the programme went beyond a set of goals and an action plan. It was this profound mindset shift that came from deep self-reflection and the connection to what's most meaningful to you – and when you see yourself with a new clarity and confidence, that inevitably leads to real-world change. The concept of the IDEA Mindset was born.

It's my vision to bring the IDEA Mindset to a wider audience. Through this book and my coaching work, I get to talk about the IDEA Mindset all the time, with friends, colleagues and clients around the world. The exercises in this book are derived from the IDEA Programme and are designed to help you find that same sense of clarity, assurance and purpose that those first coachees discovered. Alongside designing your ideal working life and creating an action plan for how to get there, the outcome of working through the exercises is to discover your IDEA Mindset, which will set you up for success and fulfilment in your future career. I hope this book will bring you as much satisfaction, clarity and fulfilment as writing it did for me!

Six Weeks to Figure Out Your Perfect Future Working Environment and Embrace Your IDEA Mindset

In the first two weeks of the programme we'll focus on figuring out what makes you tick and what your successful future career looks like. It's a career that is built around your **Identity** – who you are, what you stand for, what you're naturally brilliant at. It's a career where you're clear on your **Direction** – what your ultimate goal is, but also how you make decisions when you reach a fork in the road. And finally, you'll discover how to orientate your work around your values and core purpose, which will give you a strong sense of **Authenticity**.

In the last four weeks we'll focus on *how* you're going to reach your career goals – whether this involves a complete change of industry, going freelance, launching a flexible portfolio career, moving roles or going after the top job in your organisation – how you're going to stay there, with a plan for a working life that plays to your strengths and is designed to stimulate high **Engagement**, and how you're going to take others on the journey with you. Journeys like this always have their ups and downs. I'll be showing you how to take control of the wheel so you stay on track and arrive at your destination in one piece, while learning how to tell your story will help the people around you to offer constructive support as you design a way of working that you love.

You'll be doing some intense work here, so be ready. When you're looking to make an ambitious change, there's no space for brushing the difficult stuff under the carpet. You've got to be all in. We'll be using a wide variety of approaches to help you build resilience and unlock your potential, and reflections from some of the brightest minds of the last 100 years will help you to become more self-aware.

You'll formulate an action plan that connects end-to-end from where you are today to where you want to be in the future. We'll probe and test that plan to make sure it stands up to scrutiny and doesn't fail at the first unexpected hurdle. It will lead you to both work and a way of working that you will find intensely satisfying, that plays to your natural talents, that connects with your purpose and values.

By the end of the book, you'll have your personalised and hyper-effective action plan, you'll have started to take those first steps towards your dream future career, and in doing so you will immerse yourself in your IDEA Mindset and take ownership of what you really want from your working life.

What will your IDEA Mindset feel like?

Your IDEA Mindset isn't a certificate you can frame and put on the wall. It's not an object you can store in a box under the bed. It's something deep within you. Intangible maybe, but oh so powerful. My clients say that they have changed beyond recognition. It feels different to be them.

Your new perspective and plan will power you to a much more satisfying working life. The road won't be easy, but you'll have an inner compass to guide you on your way, and new skills and routines to support you even when the going gets tough.

The IDEA Mindset is personal to you. No one can write your vision, your purpose or your plan for you. Certainly not me! That's why in this book you have to write it for yourself. Writing is part of the journey to self-discovery and change.

There's space throughout this book for you to write, and some extra pages at the end (see page 285). I like to write by hand with one of those mechanical pencils that stays sharp, so you can also rub it out when you've changed your mind (and you will)! Iteration is the name of the game, so make it easy to tweak your scribbles as your thinking evolves.

Give your brain space and time

As well as space to write, you need time to think. This book is not some-thing to rush through. You have to allow your brain the space and time to reflect and understand. You might think you have the answer on Monday, but by Wednesday you'll have thought about it some more and you'll realise what you were missing. I often read about coaches and self-styled 'self-help gurus' offering some kind of quick fix to change your life. There is no quick fix, just as there is no such thing as a free lunch. Real change takes time. Rush through and it'll be like a crash diet – the weight will come off this week and go straight back on again next week when you drop back into your old habits.

This book is separated into weeks. In each week there is some reading and there are also some exercises to complete. The exercises might take you an hour or they might take a few hours – it depends on the nature of the exercise and how much detail you want to go into. Some of the exercises early on will take longer if they require you to talk to friends or colleagues.

However long the exercises take, remember that each week the main activity is to think. But you don't have to sit on the sofa, stare at the wall, wrinkle your brow and capital-T *Think!* if that's not how you work at your best. Create an environment where you give yourself that space and time. Allow your mind to wander when you're between tasks at work. Go out for a walk at lunchtime. Maybe sit in the park or gaze out of the window. Just let your brain be.

Our brain works best when we leave it to its own devices. All you have to do is pop the right questions in the pot – that will come from reading the book and looking at the exercises. Then stick the lid on and set the pot to a nice gentle simmer. It'll tell you when it's done.

Although I've divided the programme into weeks, you can take more time than that on the exercises if you need. If you want to go more quickly, that's also fine – but be aware that you might not have allowed your brain the time to do all its thinking. You don't want to get the roast out of the oven and find it's still raw in the middle.

You can also take time out between the weeks. You might have a clear diary one week when you can power through a set of exercises, then the following week you might be really busy. Don't force it. Remember, your brain needs the right conditions to think well. But take care not to lose momentum completely. Plan out your diary so you know when you're going to complete the week. Motivate yourself by celebrating the completion of each week. Momentum and motivation lead to action.

Is all that effort worth it? Absolutely. Unlocking your IDEA Mindset and changing your working life for the better will be transformative.

WRITE DOWN ONE THING THAT PARTICULARLY RESONATED WITH YOU FROM WHAT YOU'VE JUST READ. WHY DID YOU CHOOSE IT?

SELF-AWARENESS: The practice of becoming more aware of your thoughts and feelings — what you see, what you hear, what you feel, what you notice, what you think. Becoming more self-aware helps empower you to change your mindset. Many of the exercises in this book will help boost your self-awareness..

TAKING YOUR FIRST STEPS

You might have picked up this book because you're feeling flummoxed by the different possible career choices in front of you, paralysed by the unknown, fearful you'll mess everything up. Or you might be trying to achieve something really challenging and you're not sure yet how to tackle it. It can feel as though you're on the side of a mountain, inching along a narrow path. One wrong step could leave you slipping off the ledge.

But you're not alone.

The global pandemic has meant that a lot of people are reconsidering what's important in their work and the way they live their lives. Research from Microsoft's Work Trend Index 2021 indicates that 41 per cent of the global workforce is considering switching jobs within the next year. That's almost double the percentage of people with a similar intention in 2020.

On top of that, 2021 saw a boom in new businesses being set up – 15 per cent more than the average for the previous two years. The pandemic has given some people the opportunity to develop ideas they've been dreaming of for years.

Perhaps the unprecedented, rapid transformation in the way we work caused by the pandemic has caused you to re-evaluate what you want out of your current role or employer.

You're not alone in that either.

Employee expectations have changed. There's a new intolerance for inflexibility at work, micromanaging and target-oriented employers who make employees feel that they need to apologise for having interests or commitments outside of work, or a family. The vulnerability of this time has meant that employees are demanding more humanity and more authenticity at work. We're looking for employers who genuinely want their teams to bring their whole selves to work.

But there's only so much comfort we can take in knowing that other people are embarking on major work and life changes too. On the hard days, our path can still feel like it's being blocked by insurmountable obstacles. And on those days, what you need is the clarity and confidence to know that all you have to do is put one foot in front of the other.

That clarity and confidence is what *The IDEA Mindset* is all about.

So take that first step. Then take another. Step by step. With *The IDEA Mindset* as your guide, the climb will take care of itself.

WHAT WORDS WOULD YOU USE TO DESCRIBE YOUR WORK MINDSET TODAY?

....

....

....

....

....

....

We've already talked about how reaching your career goals and accessing your IDEA Mindset requires you to go on a journey. Sometimes it can be difficult to imagine that journey when all you have is your current frame of reference. Before Mildred and I went to train in Italy, we had no idea of what was out there and how it might impact our jobs at home. If we'd known what was possible, maybe we would have found a way to go there sooner.

If you're questioning your career choices or looking for a new challenge, I can promise you that you haven't yet unlocked your full talent. And you're not alone. These change-makers also dared to imagine a different future:

Giorgio Armani trained as a doctor and worked in a military hospital. He decided he wanted a change and found himself dressing windows at the luxury Milanese department store *La Rinascente* – the start of his journey into the fashion industry.

John Legend was a junior management consultant with the Boston Consulting Group, doing data analysis and writing PowerPoint presentations, well before his singing talents propelled him to global stardom.

Philip Pullman was a schoolteacher for 25 years before publishing the first book in the iconic *His Dark Materials* trilogy, after which he took his writing full-time.

Vera Wang was a national-level figure skater who almost qualified for the 1968 Olympic Games. When she retired from skating she retrained as a fashion journalist and eventually became the leading fashion designer she is today.

As the world-leading executive coach Marshall Goldsmith writes, 'What got you here won't get you there!' Sometimes the grass really *is* greener on the other side of the fence, if hopping over the fence unlocks your talent, your passion, your spirit, your ambition!

So, here's one really important thing you need to know. This book can help you find clarity and purpose. It can help you achieve extraordinary things in your future career, but …

THE ONLY PERSON WHO CAN ACTUALLY MAKE IT HAPPEN IS YOU.

Identity, Direction, Engagement, Authenticity

When I was growing up, we used to play a board game from the 1950s, a bit like Monopoly, called 'Careers'. In the middle of the board were a series of 'career paths' that you worked your way along.

The different careers – Farming, Business, Hollywood, Uranium, Moon – presented opportunities to win (and lose!) Money, Fame and Happiness points. Going into Business, you could earn a promotion and up your salary, but if you landed on the Too Ambitious square you got fired and ended up unemployed on the Park Bench. Going to Hollywood could make you rich and famous, but land on the Scandal square and you'd lose all your Happiness points.

You won the game by achieving your secret Success Formula, which you had to write down on a piece of paper at the start of the game. You had to amass 60 points across the categories of Money, Fame and Happiness. Some people would devise a balanced Success Formula, aiming to gain 20 points in each category. Others would put all their chips on one, pursuing 60 points of Money or Fame and forgetting all about Happiness! You had to decide what your priority was and commit to it. It's no surprise that the game was invented by a leading sociologist, Dr James Cooke Brown.

In life, as in the board game, you generally can't have everything. You can't have *all* the money, and *all* the happiness and *all* the fame. You have to decide what's important to you in real life and then go after it. For you, it might be all about happiness. Maybe you're completely motivated by money. Perhaps you just want to be famous, even if just within your industry. Or it could be that you want a bit of all three.

So how do you choose? Well, that's something that's very personal to you.

Your IDEA Mindset will underpin what you consider to be important. With your IDEA Mindset, you will fully understand who you are:

- Your **Identity**; you will have a clear sense of what your ideal future working life looks like.
- You will recognise how to get there – your **Direction**.
- You will feel fully **Engaged** with the work you're doing.
- What you do will feel **Authentic** to your values and core purpose.

When my coaching clients start the IDEA Programme, they do a simple assessment of their starting point in terms of **Identity**, **Direction**, **Engagement** and **Authenticity**. You'll complete that same assessment shortly. What is always interesting is how wide-ranging the responses are among different people when asked whether they feel a lack of clarity on their **Identity**, low **Engagement** with their work or a poor sense of **Direction** or **Authenticity**. Yet, when I ask the question, 'Was the outcome of the assessment a surprise?' the answer is invariably no. People seem to know their gaps. They just need help to fill them. That's where this book comes in.

Let's look at the four elements of your IDEA Mindset.

Identity

Your **Identity** is your sense of self. It's who you are, what you stand for and the issues that are important to you. It encompasses what your strengths are and the situations in which you excel. Your **Identity** is reflected in how others perceive you and whether that chimes with how you feel about yourself.

A strong sense of **Identity** sounds like:

- 'I'm doing the job I love and I choose to be right here doing exactly this.'
- 'I'm not surprised I enjoy my job because I'm doing things I'm really good at.'
- 'I knew what was going to come up in my performance review – both the good and the bad!'

A weak sense of **Identity** sounds like:

- 'I don't really know what kind of job I should be doing.'
- 'I don't understand why I find my job so difficult and frustrating.'
- 'I was really surprised that my team think I'm a micromanager – maybe I'm just a terrible boss.'

Direction

Your **Direction** is your clarity about the path ahead of you. It's what your long-term goals are, your big vision. It's knowing which way you'd turn when faced with a choice. Without a clear sense of **Direction**, you can feel lost in the wood and overwhelmed when you have to make decisions. You might second-guess decisions you've already made.

A strong sense of **Direction** sounds like:

- 'In a few years' time I'd really like to be running my own business.'
- 'I've been offered an opportunity to spend a year abroad. I thought about it hard, but I turned it down – it wasn't a good fit for me.'
- 'I left a job last year because I felt my progression opportunities were limited. The company did well this year and I could have got

a significant bonus if I'd stuck around for a while longer, but I made the right call for me.'

A weak sense of **Direction** sounds like:

- 'I'm still waiting for someone to offer me the role I feel I deserve. They know where I am.'
- 'I open my emails in the morning, start working through the crises and hope I get the critical stuff finished by the end of the day. I don't have the time to think about what I actually want to be doing.'
- 'I did sketch out the beginnings of a plan last year for what I wanted to achieve, but I think it ended up in one of my desk drawers. Can't remember.'

Engagement

Your **Engagement** is your level of connection with your life and work. It's how enthusiastic you are about the day ahead and how much of a sense of fulfilment you feel at the end of the day. Do you miss your work when you're not able to do it? Are you working in environments and with people who bring out the best in you? Without a good level of **Engagement**, you can feel bored or distracted, with little impetus to achieve more. You might feel like quitting because you can't face it any more, rather than quitting because you want to pursue an exciting new opportunity.

A strong sense of **Engagement** sounds like:

- 'I'm really excited about what I'm going to be doing today. This is my dream job.'
- 'I genuinely enjoy spending time with my colleagues.'
- 'I like talking with my friends outside of work about the stuff I do for a living.'

A weak sense of **Engagement** sounds like:

- 'Oh no, Monday morning again. Tuesday morning again. Wednesday morning again.'
- 'I can't think of anything much that I'm proud of doing in my work.'
- 'It's just a job. [*Checks watch*] Is it nearly time to go home yet? Just waiting for the clock to get round to the top of the hour.'

Authenticity

When your behaviour and choices connect with your values and sense of purpose, you access a deep sense of **Authenticity**. Do you feel passionate about what you do? People with a strong sense of **Authenticity** often manage their emotions well. You can make sense of even the difficult times because you're completely clear on your choices and actions. You are mindful of how the work you do impacts others and makes a difference for them. You lead with responsibility.

A strong sense of **Authenticity** sounds like:

- 'I can tell you exactly why I'm here doing what I'm doing.'
- 'I get energy from making a difference to people in need.'
- 'You can count on me to show up. If you need me to be there, I'll be there. All in.'

A weak sense of **Authenticity** sounds like:

- 'I'm just doing this for the money. One day, when I've saved up, I'll take up the career I REALLY love.' (The great delusion that there'll be a time in the future when you actually quit the well-paid job you hate!)
- 'I don't agree with some of the things we do, but it's more hassle than it's worth to mention it.'

- 'I get so frustrated all the time at work, but I don't think it would make any difference to say anything.'

When these four elements – **Identity**, **Direction**, **Engagement** and **Authenticity** – are your guiding principles, your IDEA Mindset is unlocked.

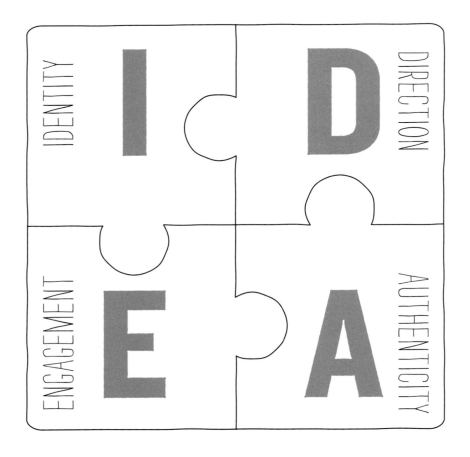

Let me be clear: this is not a science book backed up by original research. It's not the culmination of years of studying brain scans or a book informed by new psychological studies. But of course the approaches reflected in this book are tried and tested. Many of these strategies have been used in similar forms for decades to achieve extraordinary results in thousands of people.

What *is* new here is how the work I've set for you has been brought together and arranged, for maximum impact. The order in which you tackle these exercises, the conditions under which you employ these tools, the time you devote to each step of the programme, the distinctive blending of exercises to get the most out of each; all of this – the programme itself – is completely unique and targeted to deliver lasting, radical change to your working life.

This book is designed to make you think, to help you grow, to help you change. I want this to be a book you use, remember and recommend to friends and colleagues. The power and the magic of *The IDEA Mindset* is its simplicity. Something I learned throughout my career is that the best ideas are often the simplest. Einstein said, 'If you can't explain it simply, you don't understand it well enough.'

This book is simple to understand, but that doesn't mean the journey is easy. It *should* be challenging. But once you've accessed your IDEA Mindset, it's easy to hold onto. That's why I like it. You'll know when you're there and you'll never look back.

Now, let's talk about the journey you're going to go on inside your head.

Reflection

Go look in the mirror. No, really. Go look. Not just to fix your hair or admire your unimaginable beauty. Look at yourself. And keep looking. For a whole minute. Can you manage two?

Feels awkward, doesn't it? Why? Because we never do it. We don't look at ourselves. I mean, we don't *really* look at ourselves. Our eyes are pointed outwards, not inwards.

Sometimes as a coach I describe my role in the conversation as 'holding up the mirror' – helping my client to look at themselves, reflect, think about the kind of person they are and what they think about themselves. In practice I might notice and mention a particular word they used when talking about themselves, or I might comment on a change in their energy level or body language.

But I'm not there with you, so you need to be your own coach.

Be aware that when you're in self-reflection mode it can take a bit of practice to get over that initial sense of awkwardness. You might not like what you see at first. But if you don't see, then you can't understand; and if you can't understand, then you can't start to create the new mindset you're searching for.

Give yourself your undivided time and attention. Face everything there is to see and know. Don't brush anything under the carpet. This is just about you.

Take the time to reflect.

'We cannot see our reflection in running water. It is only in still water that we can see.'

TAOIST PROVERB

WRITE DOWN SIX WORDS THAT CAME INTO YOUR HEAD
WHEN YOU LOOKED AT YOURSELF IN THE MIRROR

1. ....

2. ....

3. ....

4. ....

5. ....

6. ....

The Hardest Part Is Getting Started

Is change always hard? No, not always. It's easy when you really don't like where you are today and there's no barrier to making the change you need. But if you can tolerate today and there's a high barrier between you and a better tomorrow, then making that change can be really hard. Doing nothing is almost always easier, especially when you're stressed out, tired and fed up.

Societal pressures mean we're predisposed to thinking about problems, difficulties and challenges. So, when we're thinking about the changes we need to make in our working lives, it's no wonder our internal chatter seems only to throw up all the reasons why we shouldn't bother, and what could go wrong if we tried something different.

Throughout our upbringing, voices of authority – our parents, our teachers, our first managers – might have used language focused on our weaknesses:

'Why haven't you …?'
'Why didn't you …?'
'You're supposed to …!'
'You need to …!'

These voices are demanding. They prod and poke. They create negative thought spirals. They tell us we need to fix ourselves. Like a whirlpool, they can drag us down. We can internalise these voices until the thoughts inside our own head take on the same negative tone.

But you can make hard changes feel a lot easier. The way we frame our thoughts can affect whether we feel overwhelmed or energised by the challenges and opportunities we face in our careers.

Imagine if you could change the narrative to be more focused on opportunities and strengths:

'Imagine if I just …!'
'I wonder if I could …?'
'What if I …?'
'What if we …?'

The ways these new possibilities are framed are motivating, they're exciting, they're curious, collaborative and non-judgemental. They tell us we need to stretch ourselves. They tell us to focus on our strengths and visualise our opportunities. Like a hot-air balloon, they can lift us up.

A simple change in the narrative. A dramatic impact. It's a shift that the celebrated English conductor and leadership expert Benjamin Zander articulates beautifully in his talks on YouTube. What if you could change the voices in your head to those energising ones, right now? That'll make it a whole lot easier to get started on the journey to your ideal working life. And to take control you need to start. Lots of people fail to achieve their dreams because they fail to start.

So here's the good news.

Even if all you're doing is reading this book, you've already started.

The Journey to Your IDEA Mindset

What do you need to start on this journey? Just two things. First, a copy of this book – tick! Second, a willingness to jump in with both feet.

The IDEA Mindset is about achieving real and lasting change in your working life. What's your reason for being here right now? What sparked your interest in this book over and above all other books? Hold onto that thought.

There are six steps on the journey to figuring out what your ideal working life looks like. As you take those steps, you will uncover your IDEA Mindset.

The steps work together to develop your sense of **Identity**, **Direction**, **Engagement** and **Authenticity**, through boosting your self-awareness, helping you create your plan for the future and building your personal narrative. Like baking a cake, follow the steps in the recipe and then, when you open the oven door, with a bit of luck, the whole thing has come together in a beautiful and tasty confection!

In each step there'll be exercises, thought-starters, inspiring stories, ideas and tools to help you on your journey. Remember what I said earlier

> 'We are all in the gutter, but some of us are looking at the stars.'
>
> OSCAR WILDE

about the importance of giving your brain the space and time to think (see pages 16–17)? The time you spend thinking is even more important than the time you spend reading and writing. Do the reading first so you can allow what you've learned to percolate.

YOU CAN'T THINK TO A DEADLINE.

THE IDEA MINDSET

Each week you're also going to undertake two Power Moves: focused tasks that will give you momentum as you progress through the weeks.

Finally, you'll find a suggested soundtrack to each week – three music tracks to get you in the zone. You can find all the tracks on YouTube and often I've recommended a particular version. Music has always been a big part of my life – as professional dancers, finding the right music to accompany our performance was guaranteed to bring out that extra 10–20 per cent in us. Music connects with people at a very deep level and is a great way of getting in the mood for the work you need to do.

Play the first track before you start the week's reading and exercises to get you in the right state of mind. The second track is to play on repeat in the background when you're doing your reading, thinking and writing. The third and final track is for when you're done – a celebration of completion and the uplifting energy you need to move on to the next step.

Here's a summary of what you'll be covering each week:

Week 1: Know yourself

Who are you and what do you stand for?

Where are you at your best?

When starting out on the journey to your ideal working life, it's essential to reflect on where you are today, what's important to you and what your strengths are – all critical parts of your **Identity**. You'll also think about your values, which will lay the groundwork for our thinking around **Authenticity**, which we'll be tackling throughout the programme.

You'll complete three exercises:

1. Exploring Your Values (see page 55)
2. Discovering Your Strengths (see page 62)
3. Prioritising Your Focus (see page 82)

You'll activate two Power Moves:

1. Start Your Reflective Journal (see page 86)
2. Make Progress a Daily Habit (see page 88)

Week 2: Set the course

What's the big vision?

What do you need to achieve to get there?

You need to know what your ultimate career goals are before you figure out how to reach them. Mapping out your goals, your vision and your purpose – why you choose to do what you do – will help you build a strong sense of your **Identity** and **Direction**. Only by investing your energies in a career path where that sense of purpose is deeply embedded will you feel true **Engagement** with your work and know that your work feels **Authentic** to you.

You'll complete three exercises:

1. Defining Your Vision (see page 100)
2. Defining Your Purpose (see page 105)
3. Setting Your Goals (see page 111)

You'll activate two Power Moves:

1. Share Your Vision and Purpose (see page 119)
2. Create Time to Think (see page 120)

Week 3: Prepare your mind and body for change

How will you build your mental resilience?

How can you improve your physical wellness?

Transforming your working life isn't easy, and if you want it to happen and to stick, you'll need to be in the best mental and physical shape possible. In this step you'll be reflecting on what you need to do to build your mental resilience and your physical wellbeing, and you'll start making conscious decisions that'll help your body and mind to function at their best – eating healthier foods, getting better-quality rest and incorporating movement into your daily routine. A healthy, well-rested mind and body will feel more confident, more assured and be more receptive to positive change.

You'll complete three exercises:

1. Resilience Self-assessment (see page 141)
2. Sleep Diary (see page 148)
3. Diet and Fitness Diary (see page 154)

You'll activate two Power Moves:

1. Positivity Push (see page 164)
2. Write Your Affirmation (see page 166)

Week 4: Your action plan

What do you need to do to realise your vision step by step?

What help do you need from other people?

Here you're going to create a detailed and robust action plan that will lead you to your perfect working life – whether that involves a total career change, going after a senior position in your company, adjusting your work-life balance or something totally different! In Week 2 we look at your long-term vision for what this perfect working life could look like, together with the goals you're aiming to achieve – now this is what you're going to do to make them happen. You don't have to know *exactly* what the destination is in order to be able to move things forward today. You just need to know how to make decisions in the moment.

You'll complete three exercises:

1. Creating Your Actions (see page 182)
2. Asking for Help (see page 189)
3. Drawing Up Your Timeline (see page 196)

You'll activate two Power Moves:

1. Create the Calendar (see page 204)
2. Make an Irreversible Commitment (see page 204)

Week 5: Make it stick

How can you make your new mindset a permanent
way of being, in the face of inevitable challenges?

What can you expect on the emotional journey towards radical change?

On the bumpy road of personal change, things don't always go as planned and stuff often takes longer than you might like. In this step we'll help you to maintain forward momentum and emotional **Engagement** with your career-change action plan, even in the tough times, whatever life throws at you.

You'll complete three exercises:

1. Setting Yourself Up for Success (see page 215)
2. How Will It Feel? (see page 223)
3. Escaping from the Quicksand (see page 232)

You'll activate two Power Moves:

1. Note Your Emotions (see page 233)
2. Train Your Brain (see page 234)

Week 6: Tell your story

How will you tell your story?

How will you bring others on the journey with you?

You need to be able to bring all the elements of the programme together into one coherent whole. Here, we'll be working on creating an engaging story you can tell others to describe the journey you're on. By taking people – colleagues, friends, your boss, the person interviewing you for a new job – on the journey with you, they become your supporters and your advocates, clearing the way to your perfect working life. They work with you, not against you. How do you show them that you know who you are (**Identity**), you know where you're going (**Direction**), you are enthusiastic and passionate (**Engagement**) and you're deeply, personally committed (**Authenticity**)?

You'll complete three exercises:

1. Talking Points (see page 255)
2. Building the Narrative (see page 260)
3. Testing Your Story (see page 265)

You'll activate two Power Moves:

1. Update Your Online Profiles (see page 266)
2. Network and Connect (see page 267)

That's it, the whole programme. How do you feel? Raring to go? Scared? Fired up? A bit exhausted by the thought of it all? If you're in a positive headspace and have a spare hour, throw yourself into the next task. But if you're daunted by what lies ahead, just set aside ten minutes, do as much as you can in that time, then step away. Marginal gains. You'll be surprised how much of a mood-lifter it is to do a bit of self-work.

Before we get into the detail, let's start by practising some self-reflection.

Spend five minutes sitting quietly with your thoughts.

Now write a few notes in answer to each of the following questions. Don't think too hard, just write the first thing you think of. And be honest with yourself.

'Start from wherever you are and with whatever you've got.'

JIM ROHN,
MOTIVATIONAL
SPEAKER

WHAT PROMPTED YOU TO GET A COPY OF THIS BOOK?

....

....

....

....

....

IF YOU COULD CHANGE ONE THING IN YOUR
WORKING LIFE, WHAT WOULD IT BE?

....

....

....

....

....

IF YOU COULD KEEP HOLD OF ONE THING IN YOUR
WORKING LIFE, WHAT WOULD IT BE?

....

....

....

....

....

IF YOU COULD DO ONE THING IN YOUR CAREER THAT
YOU'VE NEVER DONE BEFORE, WHAT WOULD IT BE?

....

....

....

....

....

YOUR DREAM JOB IS ...

....

....

....

....

....

THE PERSON WHO INSPIRES YOU MOST IN A WORK
CONTEXT IS (THIS CAN BE A COLLEAGUE OR A PERSON
YOU DON'T WORK DIRECTLY WITH BUT WHO YOU
FIND INSPIRING WHEN YOU'RE WORKING) ...

....

....

....

....

....

Your IDEA Profile

Let's continue with a simple questionnaire that measures how you would score yourself today against each of the IDEA elements – **Identity**, **Direction**, **Engagement**, **Authenticity**. The result of this questionnaire defines your 'IDEA Profile' and gives you a good steer as to what you need to work on to build your IDEA Mindset.

For each statement, put a tick in the appropriate column.

IDENTITY	STRONGLY AGREE	AGREE	DISAGREE	STRONGLY DISAGREE
1 I have a clear sense of what makes me unique and of what qualities I share with others				
2 I have a clear sense of my personal values				
3 I have a clear sense of how people senior to me perceive me				
4 I have a clear sense of how my peers/colleagues/ friends perceive me				
5 I have a clear sense of how people junior to me perceive me				
SCORE FOR EACH TICK	+2	+1	-1	-2
TOTAL SCORE				

DIRECTION	STRONGLY AGREE	AGREE	DISAGREE	STRONGLY DISAGREE
1 I am clear on my long-term goals				
2 I am clear on the major steps I need to take to reach them				
3 I am clear on where I am going next				
4 I have developed a simple action plan				
5 I am making good progress with my action plan				
SCORE FOR EACH TICK	+2	+1	−1	−2
TOTAL SCORE				

ENGAGEMENT	STRONGLY AGREE	AGREE	DISAGREE	STRONGLY DISAGREE
1 When I get up in the morning I am usually enthusiastic about the day ahead				
2 When I go to sleep I usually feel a sense of achievement for what I have done in the day				
3 I am doing a job that is right for me				
4 I work with people who bring out the best in me and I actively seek out people like this to work with				
5 I like to tell other people about the work I do				
SCORE FOR EACH TICK	+2	+1	-1	-2
TOTAL SCORE				

AUTHENTICITY	STRONGLY AGREE	AGREE	DISAGREE	STRONGLY DISAGREE
1 I feel a strong sense of purpose with the work I do				
2 My work aligns with my values – what I consider to be important				
3 I am emotionally engaged – I use my heart as well as my head at work				
4 I develop enduring relationships at work. I take time to listen to colleagues, clients and customers and I am sensitive to the needs of others				
5 I am disciplined in the way I work. I manage my emotions well				
SCORE FOR EACH TICK	+2	+1	-1	-2
TOTAL SCORE				

Totals

Now you've completed the questionnaire, fill in the boxes below with the total scores from each section, then calculate your total for each element.

ELEMENT	STRONGLY AGREE	AGREE	DISAGREE	STRONGLY DISAGREE	TOTAL
EXAMPLE	+4	+1	-2	0	+3
IDENTITY					
DIRECTION					
ENGAGEMENT					
AUTHENTICITY					

Interpretation

WHICH OF THE FOUR ELEMENTS DID YOU SCORE HIGHEST FOR?

....

....

WHICH ELEMENTS DID YOU GET A RELATIVELY LOW SCORE FOR?

....

....

IS THAT WHAT YOU EXPECTED OR WAS ANYTHING A SURPRISE?

....

....

....

Congratulations, that's the end of the introductory exercises. Take a breath and we'll get started with Week 1.

WEEK 1

KNOW YOURSELF

'THE WAY TO GET
STARTED IS TO
QUIT TALKING AND
BEGIN DOING.'

WALT DISNEY

E xploring who you are and what you want from your working life is at the core of this first week and key to developing a strong sense of your **Identity** – the first tenet of the IDEA Mindset. If you want to achieve real change, then you need to dedicate some quality time to thinking, planning and doing. What's quality time? It's time when you're focused, not distracted. It's time in the day when you're well rested, fed and watered. It's a big enough block of time to allow you to get some meaningful work done. Invest in quality time and you'll be repaid in how well your mindset will respond.

The commitment I want you to make to yourself is that you're going to spend the next week focused on this first step in the programme, reading, thinking and doing. You'll need to fit in the reading around whatever you're normally doing and carve out some specific time to do the exercises. The amount of time it takes will depend on your way of working and how deep your thinking is, but aim to finish this step within seven days if you can.

Mark the end of the week in your calendar now so you know what you're aiming for.

Lesson one in making change happen: just reading about it won't do it. You have to activate change. Once you've done the reading, you have to think, you have to write, you have to plan, you have to set out to achieve your goals. When Mildred and I were dancing, all the thinking in the world about how we wanted to improve our performance was worth nothing if we didn't get into the studio and put in the hours, plan for the competitions we wanted to do and follow through on our pre-planned diet and exercise regime. There are hundreds of self-help books out there which a million people read without achieving change in their lives. Make this the book that helps you make a real change in your life.

This week you can manage your 'thinking time' and 'doing time' differently.

For thinking time, you don't necessarily have to be stuck at your desk or in front of a computer screen. Sometimes the best time to think is when you're getting on with normal life – maybe commuting to work, walking the dog or doing the laundry. Stick this book in your pocket or your bag and, as you're reading through the exercises, scribble thoughts and ideas in the margins or at the back of the book (see page 285) as they come into your head. Or read up on what you need to do at the beginning of the week and jot down thoughts on your phone as they come to you.

THROW YOUR THOUGHTS INTO THE POT, POP THE LID ON, ALLOW TO SIMMER AND DON'T PEEK UNTIL THEY'RE DONE.

THE IDEA MINDSET

After you've devoted some time to *thinking* about your responses to the exercises, you need to spend some time writing up your answers. That's when you want to find yourself a quiet corner for an hour or so, free of distractions. You need a block of time when you can allow your brain to settle. Settling is important. It's difficult to jump from a stressful meeting straight into doing some deep self-reflection. You need to give your brain some time to reduce the rev count and switch gears.

There are three exercises you're going to complete this week.

We'll start with **Exploring Your Values** (see page 55), which will uncover those inherent truths that define who you are, what matters to you and what drives your choices.

Next, we'll move on to **Discovering Your Strengths** (see page 62), which will reveal what you're best at and where you're naturally inclined. Aligning your plan with your natural talents and strengths is like running with the wind behind you – it makes it easier to win your race.

Finally, we're going to look at **Prioritising Your Focus** (see page 82). In my experience, you're much more likely to succeed in achieving your career goals if you focus on making a small number of high-impact changes rather than lots of little changes. As I sometimes say to my clients, if you only have time to make one step forward, make it a big one.

At the end of each week you'll also undertake two Power Moves. A Power Move is a targeted exercise to help accelerate you on your journey. It's the beginning of the New You. This week your two Power Moves are:

1. Start Your Reflective Journal (see page 86)
2. Make Progress a Daily Habit (see page 88)

SOUNDTRACK TO YOUR WEEK

This week's soundtrack is about identity, connection and commencement.

Play this track before you start the week's reading and exercises to get you in the mood: '*Schindler's List* – Theme' by John Williams. Watch the version played by the Netherlands Symphony Orchestra in 2018. Cor anglais player Davida Scheffers suffers from a medical condition that cut short her professional playing career, but on the day of this performance she realised her dream of playing this beautiful piece with the orchestra for her daughter on her eighteenth birthday – the whole performance is a real emotional journey.

Play this track on repeat in the background while you're doing your reading, thinking and writing: '*Interstellar* Main Theme' by Hans Zimmer. This cinematic tour-de-force from 2014 will help open your mind to truly epic levels. Hans Zimmer's music is fabulous to have playing in the background when you want to focus or study.

Play this track when you're done, in celebration of completion and to provide the uplifting energy you need to move on to the next step: 'This Is Me' by Keala Settle. The anthem from the film *The Greatest Showman* (2017) will fill you with positivity as you reflect on your power and strength. Find the version they filmed in the pre-production workshop, where you get the raw, unbridled passion of Keala's original performance.

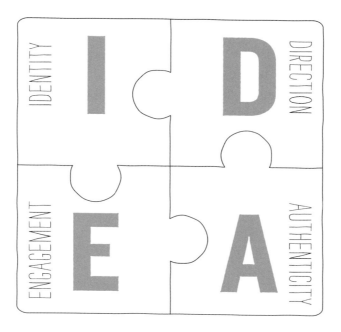

Exercise I: Exploring Your Values

When Mildred and I first arrived in Italy, facing our big decision – whether to be bold and risk our day jobs, sanity, stability and solvency or to quit our ballroom dancing career – we asked ourselves the question: 'Why would we turn our lives upside-down to pursue this dream?' We realised that it all came down to three shared values. One: persistence. We were not done with our journey. We were not the kind of people who quit halfway up the mountain. Two: adaptability. If the route to the top required us to throw away everything we had built and start again from scratch, so be it. We were not sentimental types. Three: non-conformity. We liked being the rebels who quit the system and forged our own path. No one expected us to succeed. We were energised by that challenge.

Before our dance career, I hadn't particularly thought of myself as a values-led person. Since retiring, I have been far more mindful of who I am and what makes me tick. It's why I decided to pursue coaching as my full-time occupation, passing on other opportunities that I would have been good at but wouldn't have loved. I'm comfortable with the decisions I've made and I don't worry about what might have been.

We all have values that we believe in. Courage or humility. Honesty or generosity. Your values are the guiderails to the way you live your whole life, the choices you make, the interactions you have with others. They reflect your view on what's right and wrong and they affect your behaviour.

Many people discover their values through experience. We notice how we feel when something particularly good or bad happens to us. We notice what considerations come into play when we're faced with a tough choice. It's common not to know what your values are until you're placed in a particularly joy-filled or high-stress situation that makes them glaringly apparent!

A true value will prompt you to do something, or perhaps stop doing something. If you don't act differently because of it, it's not really a value. For example, you might choose to turn down a high-paying role that would require you to work weekends because you value your free time or time with your family and friends. Or you might move to a new location to work with an organisation you admire because of what they stand for.

We can all probably name some people we know who we think have strong values. The friend who volunteers every weekend at the food bank. The colleague who raised the topic of workplace bullying to support others she felt didn't have a voice. The sustainability entrepreneur who turned down an investor because they didn't really believe in the mission and purpose of the company. But values don't have to be the same as having a strong social conscience. Quality is a value. Professionalism is a value. Adventure is a value. Fun is a value.

If you can identify and clearly articulate your values, that's an important first step to building your sense of **Identity**.

Last time you had to make a big decision, what drove your choice? What are the characteristics and behaviours you like to see in your friends and colleagues? What behaviours in other people really bug you? What does that say about what's important to you?

> 'Values are like fingerprints. Nobody's are the same, but you leave them all over everything you do.'
>
> **ELVIS PRESLEY**

Write down below four to six words that you think reflect your values. The words should be specific and meaningful for you – read them back, and if you find they could describe pretty much anyone, then think of some different ones.

Next, think about whether those values genuinely drive your life choices and behaviours. Can you think of a time when you decided to do something, or decided not to do something, because of each value?

WORDS THAT REFLECT YOUR VALUES:

....

....

....

WRITE DOWN A TIME WHEN YOUR ACTIONS
WERE DETERMINED BY YOUR VALUES:

....

....

....

....

Now let's delve into some situations that might help you clarify and refine these values. Your values can shine through in positive situations, and you might also notice their absence in situations that felt very negative for you.

When you're having a positive experience that you go on to store in your long-term memory bank, it often means one of your core values was notably present during that experience. Maybe you'd been recognised for doing something outstanding at work. Maybe you were working with a team to achieve something extraordinary. Maybe it was something you observed someone else doing that made you think and reflect. What does that tell you about yourself?

THINK OF A MEANINGFUL POINT IN YOUR CAREER OR
PERSONAL LIFE. DESCRIBE IT AND LIST THE VALUES
THAT WERE FULLY PRESENT IN THAT MOMENT:

....

....

....

....

....

....

....

....

'If you don't stick to your
values when they are being
tested, they're not values:
they're hobbies.'

JON STEWART,
COMEDIAN, WRITER
AND TV PERSONALITY

When something happens that triggers negative emotions – frustration, anger, anxiety – it is often an indicator that your values are being trampled on. Maybe you've put your faith in someone and they've let you down. Maybe you've seen someone putting themselves first at the expense of their colleagues. Maybe you've seen someone walk on by when you think you'd have stopped to help. What does that tell you about yourself?

THINK OF A TIME WHEN YOU EXPERIENCED NEGATIVE EMOTIONS – FRUSTRATION, ANGER, ANXIETY – IN YOUR CAREER OR PERSONAL LIFE. DESCRIBE IT AND THEN LIST THE VALUES YOU WERE BETRAYING OR FELT WERE NOT BEING EXHIBITED IN THAT MOMENT:

....

....

....

....

....

....

....

Reflecting on your responses to these questions, pick out the values that are *truly essential* to your existence, that are relevant when you make the big choices in life – when you say yes to things and also when you say no to things. What are the values that show up again and again in those meaningful moments?

Now create your Personal Values Statement. This could just be a list of values, or you might like to write something a bit more personal and meaningful for you.

For example: 'My values are quality, equality and honesty. I am energised by delivering high-quality work and I strive always to deliver work that meets my high standards, even if I need to compromise on other things to achieve that (such as speed). I care that people are treated equally and fairly and I am learning all the time about how I can sometimes be biased. It's important to me that I can be honest with the people around me and that I can trust that they will be honest with me. If they aren't able to do that, I have to consider the possibility that we shouldn't be in each other's lives.'

PERSONAL VALUES STATEMENT

A sentence or paragraph describing the values that are most important to you in your life.

YOUR PERSONAL VALUES STATEMENT:

....

....

....

....

Take the time to think about these values. Feel free to come back to this exercise later and tweak them if you need to. These are the foundations for your IDEA Mindset. They should be strong and stable.

Exercise 2: Discovering Your Strengths

Why do so many of us live our lives feeling like imposters, worrying about whether we're going to be caught out for something we can't do or something we've messed up?

It's in our nature to focus on our faults and our failures, ingrained from when our homework came back covered in red pen. My school report for French contained the diplomatic feedback, 'Guesses sensibly.' I don't think it was meant as a compliment, even though it turned out to be a very powerful life skill! Life is full of people telling us what we're doing wrong and how to fix it. People often feel more in control when pointing out someone else's faults.

'You need to get better at being organised.'

'I noted a couple of errors on your slides.'

'You should really smarten yourself up for work.'

'Why can't you be more like your colleague?'

Most of us don't spend enough time telling each other when we've done something well or are good at something. Positive psychology can often be dismissed as 'soft' or 'touchy-feely'. Yet our talents and strengths are our superpowers. They're what we're best at, what we find easiest, what we pick up quickly, what we love to do. Why shouldn't we celebrate that? Why shouldn't we lean into that?

'You're really good at summarising what's important.'

'That was a great piece of analysis you did –
now it's clear what we need to do next.'

'People feel so motivated when they've spent time with you.'

'I really liked how you handled that situation.'

> # FREEDOM IS THE DAY YOU REALISE THAT IT'S OK NOT TO BE GOOD AT EVERYTHING. CHOOSE THE PATH THAT PLAYS TO YOUR STRENGTHS.
>
> ## THE IDEA MINDSET

Imagine that you'd spent your childhood learning to play the flute – you were some kind of flute prodigy and made it sound like the music of angels. Now you're auditioning for the school orchestra and someone hands you a violin, and then chastises you when you can't make it sound like anything other than a screeching cat! That's what it's like when we spend our lives focusing on our faults. We're playing the wrong instrument. Put down the violin. Pick up the flute. You'll be happier and everyone else will be thankful, too.

You can spend your life trying to fix your faults, and you can go from poor to average or even quite good. But if it's not a natural talent, then it's a much harder road to true excellence, however much time and effort you put in. Or you can recognise your natural talents and strengths and orientate your life to play to them. That way, you'll find things easier, you'll be more engaged with what you're doing, your work will be more closely aligned with your values and you'll achieve much bigger goals.

Analytics and advisory firm Gallup, whose CliftonStrengths talent assessment is used globally by companies wanting to unlock the innate potential of their employees (see page vii), has done extensive research on strengths and weaknesses. They define a weakness as 'anything that gets in the way of your strengths'. They believe there is no such thing as fixing a weakness, only managing it. And the way to manage a weakness is to use your strengths.[2]

A talent

Something you are naturally good at, that you pick up quickly, you really enjoy doing and which, with the investment of time and effort, you can turn into a high-level skill. Example: You have a musical ear and you love listening to and performing music.

A strength

The result of investing time and effort in becoming great at doing something for which you probably already had a natural talent. Example: You're skilled and experienced in developing and motivating a team, and your teams recognise you as an excellent leader and coach.

A weakness

Something that you're not good at but which you need to be good at in your chosen life. Example: You're not good at taking exams, but you need a finance qualification to progress. You might manage this weakness by using your influencing strength to convince your boss to send you on a suitable course. If you don't need to use that skill in your work, then don't think of it as a weakness, just think of it as something that 'isn't you'.

Your natural talents and strengths are a core part of your **Identity**. Shaping your life choices around your strengths is like choosing to cycle down the hill instead of up it. Gravity works with you, not against you.

Of course, there's a place for building up the skills that don't come so naturally but which would nevertheless be valuable to have in your line of work; for instance, public speaking. You might want to consider taking steps to proactively develop these skills, particularly if those areas of weakness trip you up in life or work.

You can win in life by being really clear about those areas where you naturally shine, and then playing to those strengths. And in this exercise, you have two options to help you do this. For the most rigorous and reliable results, I recommend that you complete Gallup's CliftonStrengths 34 sophisticated psychometric talent assessment, which you can purchase online (see below). Or, if you prefer, complete the alternative exercise on page 67 that will give a much simpler but still useful idea of your strengths.

Complete CliftonStrengths® 34

To get a good understanding of your strengths, take the CliftonStrengths psychometric assessment (see page vii). You don't have to take the test to get the most out of this book, but it's a useful tool. Search online for 'Gallup CliftonStrengths 34' and you will find the page on the Gallup website where you can purchase a code to complete this multiple-choice test.

I am a Gallup-certified Strengths Coach and have used the CliftonStrengths assessment with my coaching clients for many years. The kinds of strengths identified by CliftonStrengths include:

Activator® – you're someone who turns thoughts into action. When others are still talking, you're the one getting going. You get frustrated by people wasting time.

Maximizer® – you have a real talent for taking things that are already good and making them great. You're much more energised by this than by improving weaknesses.

Restorative® – you are brilliant at dealing with problems by figuring out what is wrong and fixing it. You hate ignoring a problem.

There are 34 different talent themes and the assessment ranks them in order, then offers you personalised and practical insights on your talents and how to use them to be more successful and fulfilled in the future. There is also a lower-cost version (CliftonStrengths Top 5) that gives you a short summary of your top five strengths.

Complete the CliftonStrengths assessment online, read your reports and then answer the questions below. There is space here for your top three strengths and you can do the same activity for more of your strengths on a separate piece of paper if you find it helpful.

Alternative approach to discovering your strengths

If you'd rather not take the CliftonStrengths assessment, you can follow the simple steps below and use these to fill in the next exercises as a basic indicator of your strengths. This alternative exercise is not based on Gallup's extensive scientific and statistical analysis. However, it's a simple tool to help you think about what you're good at.

Take a look at the following simple phrases, which describe a range of natural abilities. There are some blank spaces for adding any that you feel are missing.

CREATING NEW THINGS	MAKING CHANGE HAPPEN	HELPING OTHERS	ANALYSING DATA
SOLVING DIFFICULT PROBLEMS	GIVING DIRECTION	MAKING PEOPLE HAPPY	GETTING THINGS FINISHED
TELLING STORIES	MAKING PLANS	MAKING DECISIONS	DOING THINGS CAREFULLY
BRINGING PEOPLE TOGETHER	MENDING THINGS THAT ARE BROKEN	LEARNING	MEETING DEADLINES

Now answer the following questions and also ask someone who knows you well to take the time to tell you what they think. Use the answers from the last row in the next part of the exercise.

	WHAT I THINK	WHAT MY COLLEAGUE THINKS
The three activities, from among those listed, that I'm naturally best at are:		
Three activities that I find easier than other people to do well are:		
The three activities I find most enjoyable are:		
My top three strengths according to the answers above are:		

Assessing your strengths

Complete the following section for your top strengths, as determined by either your CliftonStrengths assessment or the simplified exercise above.

STRENGTH 1: _____

READ THE DESCRIPTION OF THIS STRENGTH IN YOUR CLIFTONSTRENGTHS REPORT OR, IF YOU COMPLETED THE SIMPLIFIED EXERCISE, THINK ABOUT ITS DEFINITION. WHAT WORDS IN THAT DESCRIPTION PARTICULARLY RESONATE WITH YOU?

....

....

....

....

....

DESCRIBE AN EPISODE YOU'RE PROUD OF WHEN YOU'VE MADE/YOU MAKE GOOD USE OF THIS STRENGTH. THIS CAN BE A SINGLE INCIDENT OR RECURRING POINTS THROUGHOUT YOUR EVERYDAY LIFE:

....

....

....

....

WHAT COULD YOU DO DIFFERENTLY TO MAKE GREATER USE OF THIS STRENGTH IN FUTURE?

....

....

....

....

....

STRENGTH 2: _____

READ THE DESCRIPTION OF THIS STRENGTH IN YOUR CLIFTONSTRENGTHS REPORT OR, IF YOU COMPLETED THE SIMPLIFIED EXERCISE, THINK ABOUT ITS DEFINITION. WHAT WORDS IN THAT DESCRIPTION PARTICULARLY RESONATE WITH YOU?

....

....

....

....

....

DESCRIBE AN EPISODE YOU'RE PROUD OF WHEN YOU'VE MADE/YOU MAKE GOOD USE OF THIS STRENGTH. THIS CAN BE A SINGLE INCIDENT OR RECURRING POINTS THROUGHOUT YOUR EVERYDAY LIFE:

....

....

....

....

WHAT COULD YOU DO DIFFERENTLY TO MAKE GREATER USE OF THIS STRENGTH IN FUTURE?

....

....

....

....

....

STRENGTH 3: _____

READ THE DESCRIPTION OF THIS STRENGTH IN YOUR
CLIFTONSTRENGTHS REPORT OR, IF YOU COMPLETED
THE SIMPLIFIED EXERCISE, THINK ABOUT ITS
DEFINITION. WHAT WORDS IN THAT DESCRIPTION
PARTICULARLY RESONATE WITH YOU?

....

....

....

....

....

DESCRIBE AN EPISODE YOU'RE PROUD OF WHEN YOU'VE
MADE/YOU MAKE GOOD USE OF THIS STRENGTH.
THIS CAN BE A SINGLE INCIDENT OR RECURRING
POINTS THROUGHOUT YOUR EVERYDAY LIFE:

....

....

....

....

WHAT COULD YOU DO DIFFERENTLY TO MAKE
GREATER USE OF THIS STRENGTH IN FUTURE?

....

....

....

....

....

Gather feedback on you at your best

It's easy to make assumptions about what other people think of us, particularly when we're feeling under pressure or overwhelmed. We can start to believe things that aren't true. When I'm talking with my clients, they often say things like, 'Actually, that conversation went better than I was expecting,' or, 'They said some really nice things about me!' Positive, constructive feedback is a helpful way to reconnect us with reality when we're in a negative thought spiral, but honestly, we should give and receive more of it every day! It's a critical part of how we learn and grow.

Here, we're focusing on feedback explicitly to help you understand and activate your strengths, which in turn will help you gain clarity on your **Identity**. Often people equate feedback with 'highlighting areas for improvement' – but here we're zoning in on the positives.

'The key to learning is feedback. It's nearly impossible to learn anything without it.'
STEVEN LEVITT, ECONOMIST

STRENGTHS-FOCUSED FEEDBACK

Thoughts and opinions that help you reflect and build on your strengths instead of obsessing about fixing your weaker areas.

When Mildred and I were dancers, feedback was incredibly important. In a visual artform, there can be a big gap between what *you're* feeling and how you're making *others* feel. Feedback could come in many forms. We could get a video recording of our performance or direct feedback from the audience on the day. Sometimes we'd get feedback days or even weeks after the event. This was always particularly interesting, as the memorable aspects of our performance told us a lot about where we were most impactful.

One of the great life lessons our dance coach Davide taught me was: 'Listen for what they saw, not what they think you should do differently. If they say, "You should lean more to the right," then you should think, "They have seen that there is something wrong with my posture." They might not use the words "there is something wrong with your posture". Then look at the video to find the problem. Sometimes people have a good eye, but because they don't know you and what you are working on, they might not give you good advice on what to do differently.'

It was a great insight and it's something that I come back to often with my coaching clients. You have to listen beyond the direct feedback in order to extract its usefulness, then decide for yourself what you want to do about it. And remember, it's perfectly OK to listen to the feedback and choose not to change anything. That's you taking ownership of your decisions and their consequences.

I've had times in my corporate career since retiring from dancing when I've had people tell me what they think I should do to either be more successful in my role or to be considered for promotion. Often, I've made suggestions that my colleagues didn't want to hear because it meant accepting that big changes were needed, and I wouldn't sugar-coat what I felt needed to be said. I was told to compromise, keep quiet and play the long game. Sometimes I've taken that advice and sometimes I've reflected on it and chosen a different path. Ultimately, it's my decision and it's for me to live with the consequences. I've never regretted being authentic.

Using the questionnaire below, get feedback on your strengths from at least three people so you have a variety of opinions to reflect on. You should pick people who know you well; they don't necessarily have to be work colleagues. Think about approaching:

- People who have had the opportunity to observe your style and approach fairly closely in a work setting over at least six months in the last two to three years. They might be more senior than you, on the same level or more junior, but not necessarily directly managing or reporting into you, and they'll have witnessed how you work with others at different levels.
- People who have seen you in both positive and more challenging situations.
- People who are honest and trustworthy, and who are prepared to give you a rounded and fair view without being scared to tell you what they really think!

Getting feedback from people may take more than a few days. Bearing in mind your goal to complete this week's activities within seven days, it's fine to kick off the process this week and then work through the feedback down the line if it comes back a bit later.

Personal feedback questionnaire

Where I'm most comfortable

1. What activities do you think I'm instinctively drawn to?
2. What activities do you think I particularly enjoy?
3. What activities do I seem to pick up easily?
4. What activities do I perform to a particularly high level?
5. What activity can I get completely lost in?

Me at work

1. Describe a situation in which I work at my best.
2. What words would people who work with me use to describe me?
3. Do I bring out the best in the people I work with? How?
4. How do you think I feel about work? Why do you say that?
5. Do you think I am a good influencer? Why do you say that?

My energy

1. How would you describe my energy level at work?
2. Do you think I have a strong sense of purpose? How would you describe it?
3. Am I a good listener? What makes you say that?
4. What triggers stress in me and do I handle it well?
5. What one thing do you suggest I start doing that I don't do today?

Ask for the person's feedback in written form. That will encourage them to think their answers through carefully and to be specific. You might also wish to have a phone or video call with them (perhaps ask if you can record it) or a chat over coffee to talk it through. If you receive verbal feedback or clarification, then add notes to what they've written so that you have a record of all the feedback for future reference.

Reflect on the feedback

Once you've received your feedback, think through the following questions and make some notes.

DID THINGS COME UP THAT YOU WERE EXPECTING TO HEAR?

....

....

....

....

....

DID ANYTHING COME UP THAT YOU WERE SURPRISED
TO HEAR? IF SO, WHAT AND WHY?

....

....

....

....

....

DID DIFFERENT PEOPLE GIVE YOU CONFLICTING
VIEWS? WHAT DO YOU THINK THAT TELLS YOU?

....

....

....

....

....

WERE THERE COMMON THEMES YOU THINK
YOU OUGHT TO REFLECT ON?

....

....

....

....

....

WAS THERE ANYTHING YOU'D LIKE TO GO BACK
AND CLARIFY OR DISCUSS FURTHER?

....

....

....

....

Exercise 3: Prioritising Your Focus

Steve Jobs said, 'Do not try to do everything. Do one thing well.' As we start to determine our **Direction** – essentially the long-term plan and the foundation for strong decision-making – focus is one of our most valuable skills. When we feel that life is out of control, it can often mean that we have lost our focus. Does any of this feel familiar?

'There are a million things going on.'

'I'm super-busy but I don't feel as though I'm making much progress.'

'I can't see the wood for the trees.'

In this exercise, you're going to identify and prioritise your career focus areas. Think about the 80:20 rule – 80 per cent of the benefit will come from 20 per cent of the work you put in.

What do you want to happen? What do you need to change?

> 'Most people have no idea of the giant capacity we can immediately command when we focus all of our resources on mastering a single area of our lives.'
>
> TONY ROBBINS, LIFE AND BUSINESS COACH

A need

A need is an outcome you need to achieve or something you need to change. A need could be something you need to *have*, or need to *do*, or need to *stop doing*. It could be something you need *more of*, or something you need *less of*.

In the context of the IDEA Mindset, think of a need as a current ongoing problem that's impacting the quality of your working life, and which requires a solution.

Here are some examples to give you an idea of what a need sounds like:

- I **need** to switch off more at the weekends.
- I **need** to be more assertive at work.
- I **need** to achieve a better work-life balance.
- I **need** to sort out that long to-do list.
- I **need** to improve my finance skills.
- I **need** to stop getting so stressed before big meetings.
- I **need** to feel more confident when I present.
- I **need** to get more routine in my daily life.

Get yourself a piece of scrap paper. Read back through the notes and comments you've made through the process so far. Remember why you chose to go on this journey. Think about what you need to build, or what needs to change. Then read the list of example needs above. Think about whether any of these resonate with you or whether your needs are different.

Now write down the ten most important needs in your working life in full sentences, like the examples above. Don't worry about the order at this stage.

THE MOST IMPORTANT NEEDS IN YOUR WORKING LIFE:

1. I NEED TO ....

2. I NEED TO ....

3. I NEED TO ....

4. I NEED TO ....

5. I NEED TO ....

6. I NEED TO ....

7. I NEED TO ....

8. I NEED TO ....

9. I NEED TO ....

10. I NEED TO ....

Next, you're going to make some decisions about which needs you want to focus on addressing. This could be just one, or maybe two or three, but probably no more than six or seven. To help you work out which of your needs are the most important, try using the Golden Spiral of Needs below. Using your list of ten needs, write one of them in each segment below. Your most important need should go in the biggest segment, your second-most important should go in the second-biggest segment, and so on.

You will naturally find that you have to make difficult choices. Not all of your needs will fit. You will have to choose which ones to focus on.

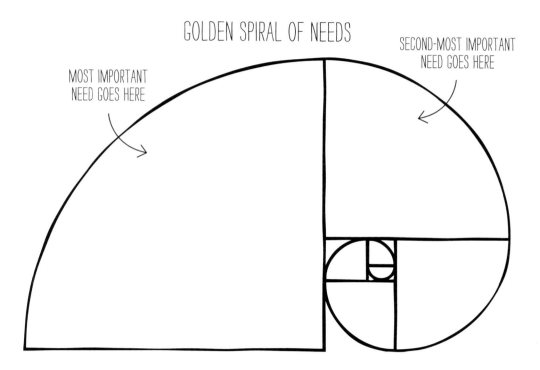

GOLDEN SPIRAL OF NEEDS

MOST IMPORTANT NEED GOES HERE

SECOND-MOST IMPORTANT NEED GOES HERE

The 'and the rest' list

If there are any of your needs that still feel really important but you couldn't fit them on your Golden Spiral of Needs, feel free to write them below. Give yourself a bonus point if you can leave this next section empty!

NEEDS IN YOUR WORKING LIFE THAT YOU COULDN'T BEAR
TO LEAVE OUT OF THE GOLDEN SPIRAL OF NEEDS:

....

....

....

....

....

Good job! Having your Golden Spiral of Needs should give you real clarity and focus on where you want to spend your time and energy as you work through the next few weeks. This will help prepare you to define your **Direction**.

You might want to take a photo of your Golden Spiral of Needs and pin it up on the wall or make it the desktop background on your computer, as a reminder.

Power Move I: Start Your Reflective Journal

A Power Move is a targeted exercise at the end of each week. This isn't just planning any more; this is you taking action, bringing you closer to your ideal work set-up. The feeling of achievement you'll get from completing your Power Move will accelerate you on your journey.

This book is the compass helping you to find your IDEA Mindset, but it can't tell you what your perfect working life looks like.

Why not?

Because you contain all the answers.

Think about that for a minute. **You contain all the answers.**

All we need to do is get at them, and that requires self-reflection.

A Reflective Journal is a way of scribbling down what you're thinking or feeling as you go through your journey. Thoughts are fleeting. Writing in a journal helps to capture your own valuable nuggets of insight and enables you to look back and see how you're changing, growing and progressing over the weeks, building self-awareness as you go.

To start your Reflective Journal, all you need is something to write on and something to write with. No laptops, no phones – you should be free of distractions; just you and your thoughts.

You might want to write about:

- How you felt at the start of the process.
- What you were thinking when you started to do the exercises.
- Things that came up which you weren't expecting.
- Interesting questions you are asking yourself.
- Places where you are starting to find new clarity and direction.
- A situation at work you responded to differently than usual.
- A conversation with a colleague that was different than usual.
- How you're feeling having completed the exercises.
- Thoughts you'd like to come back to.

When you're starting out, try to write something in the journal every day. As you get into the programme, feel free to write as much or as little as is helpful for you. But don't wait – get started right now!

Power Move 2: Make Progress a Daily Habit

This Power Move is about turning the fundamental actions of personal change into habits. A habit is a regular practice that's hard to give up. You want to make progress towards your perfect working life a habit – that'll help you maintain momentum even when you lose focus or feel dispirited. Everyone has hard days, and good habits help on those days.

Here, we're going to identify one thing you're going to start doing as a new routine. Think about your top strength from the Discovering Your Strengths exercise (see page 62) and your number one priority from your Golden Spiral of Needs (see page 85). Can you figure out a way to blend the two into a super-effective habit, answering a career need with a strength? Or perhaps you'd like to formulate a habit that taps into either a current need or a strength.

Here are some examples of habits that might help you address a need or use a strength:

- Make a plan for the day over breakfast and highlight your top three priorities so you are clear on your focus.
- Block out regular time in your diary to develop a skill that will help you at work.
- Do your least favourite activity first so it's out of the way and you can enjoy the rest of your day.

WHAT STRENGTH AND/OR NEED DO YOU WANT TO TARGET?

....

....

....

WHAT NEW HABIT ARE YOU COMMITTING TO?

....

....

....

Week 1: Know Yourself – Reflections

In this first week you've been focusing on **Identity** and working up some initial thoughts that will lay the groundwork for your career **Direction**.

Have you learned anything new about yourself? Do you feel clearer about who

'A journey of a thousand miles starts with a single step.'
LAO TZU, PHILOSOPHER

you are, how to bring out the best in yourself and what you want to achieve on this journey?

Lean into the process of allowing the thinking and the work you've done this week to evolve as you move through the programme. Change your needs if you realise they no longer apply. Tweak your daily habit if it doesn't serve you. Revisit your values if you realise you've left something crucial out. Your work, opinions and goals are not set in stone.

'Embrace uncertainty. Some of the most beautiful chapters in our lives won't have a title until much later.'

BOB GOFF,
MOTIVATIONAL SPEAKER

Your IDEA Mindset: self-reflection

At the end of each week, you're going to score yourself on how far you think you've progressed on each of the IDEA Mindset components compared with where you were at the start of the week. Remember the definitions:

Identity

Clarity about who you are, what you stand for and the issues that are important to you. What your strengths are and the situations in which you excel. How others perceive you and whether that chimes with how you feel about yourself. A sense of self-assurance, an inner compass.

Direction

Clarity about the path ahead of you, what your long-term career goals are and knowing which way you'd turn when faced with a choice. Making forward progress along the path to your perfect career. A sense of comfort with the decisions you've made.

Engagement

Your level of connection with your life and work. How enthusiastic you are about the day ahead and how much of a sense of fulfilment you feel at the end of the day. You are excited about possible career opportunities ahead. Maybe you can see a path to a situation you'd love to be in.

Authenticity

Clarity about how your behaviour and choices at work connect with your values and sense of purpose. Your level of emotional connection with your life and work. Your passion. You're clear on why you're doing what you're doing, or, if not, you're starting to shape a path to an authentic future career.

Put a plus symbol in the appropriate box of the diagram below if you think you've moved forward on one or more of these IDEA Mindset components with the work you've done this week. Put more than one plus if you think you've moved forward a lot. Think about the way you've felt at work, and about the conversations you've had with friends and colleagues. Do you think your mindset is changing?

Example:

Now it's your turn:

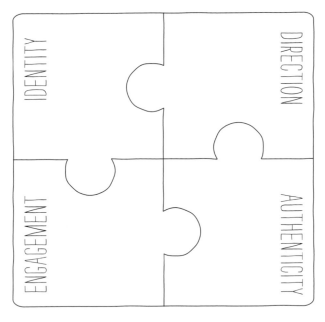

Phew! That's it.

Rest up so you're ready for Week 2.

> TAKEAWAY THOUGHT: Relax and enjoy the journey. Give yourself the time to work on your own growth. You deserve to take that time.

WEEK 2

SET THE COURSE

You've built some strong foundations in Week 1, exploring the different elements of your **Identity** and beginning to focus on your **Direction**. Now it's time to get going on what you can see above ground to develop that sense of **Direction** further, which in turn will lead to greater **Engagement** and **Authenticity** in the future.

This week, you're going to imagine your ideal future and map out what it looks like – that's your vision. You're going to think about what gets you out of bed in the morning and makes you feel fulfilled – that's your purpose. And finally, you're going to think about the things you actually need to build to make all that happen – those are your goals. Your vision, your purpose and your goals will be the anchor points for your action plan. We'll be drawing that up in detail later.

Imagine you're building a house. Before you even draw up the plans, you'd ask yourself some big questions. What style of house do I like? How much space do I want? How many bedrooms? What will I be doing in the house – working? Cooking? Will it need to be child-friendly?

You might imagine yourself in the house, waking up in the morning and getting yourself ready, or coming home in the evening and spending time with your family. Thinking about living in the space will help you work out how to design it.

Figuring out what you want your working life to look like and how you'll get there is a bit like building this house.

It seems like it might be easy. It isn't. For sure, there are some people who have their house planned out from childhood, but equally there are plenty of people – me included – who took a good amount of

> 'The two most important days in your life are the day you are born and the day you find out why.'
>
> MARK TWAIN

time to work out what they wanted their house to look like. There's no right answer, there's only what's right for you. Remember those examples of people who found their true calling later in their careers (see page 20).

There are three exercises you're going to complete this week.

We'll start with **Defining Your Vision** (see page 100). This is big-picture stuff – your future working life and dream career. The destination. What will your daily life look like once you're doing your perfect job in exactly the way you want to be doing it?

Then we'll move on to **Defining Your Purpose** (see page 105). What gets you out of bed every morning? What's your passion? What energises you?

Finally, we're going to be **Setting Your Goals** (see page 111). Your goals are the specific, real-world components that make up your vision. In essence, they're the objectives you will have met when you realise your career vision.

Just like last week, we're going to finish the week with your Power Moves, those targeted exercises to help accelerate you on your journey. This week your two Power Moves are:

1. Share Your Vision and Purpose (see page 119)
2. Create Time to Think (see page 120)

SOUNDTRACK TO YOUR WEEK

This week's soundtrack is about embracing your uniqueness and finding your purpose.

Play this track before you start the week's reading and exercises to get you in the mood: 'People Help the People' by Birdy. An inspirational cover sung by Birdy at the tender age of 15 about the need to help one another.

Play this track on repeat in the background when you're doing your reading, thinking and writing: '*Comptine d'un autre été*' by Yann Tiersen. You'll recognise this as the theme from the film *Amélie*, in which Audrey Tautou plays the shy Parisian waitress who makes it her mission to change the lives of those around her in a delightfully quirky way.

Play this track when you're done, in celebration of completion and to provide the uplifting energy you need to move on to the next step: 'Brave' by Sara Bareilles. Inspired by a close friend coming out as gay, this uplifting anthem from 2013 celebrates people being who they are and speaking honestly.

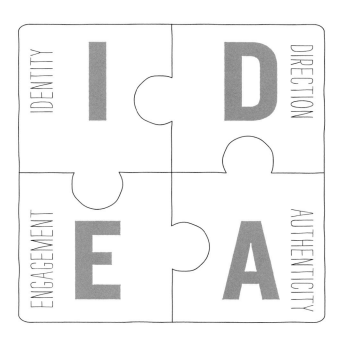

Exercise 1: Defining Your Vision

A great vision is a simple and inspirational articulation of your perfect working life. It gives you motivation. It gives you **Direction**. Without a vision, you're like a pinball, pinging all over the pinball machine. You might be racking up points, but you're hardly in control! Your vision is the anchor point for your whole plan, so it's worth spending some time getting it right. Everything you do should build towards your vision, or at least not detract from it.

Your vision doesn't have to be perfectly formed or sharply in focus, but if you have some idea of where you want to end up, it helps you make decisions in the short term.

> 'The only person you are destined to become is the person you decide to be.'
>
> RALPH WALDO EMERSON, ESSAYIST AND PHILOSOPHER

Sometimes your vision will involve you taking yourself outside your comfort zone. It might be about quitting your job and setting up your own business. It might be about putting yourself in a high-profile position, where your successes and strengths are more visible, but then again so are your weaknesses and failings! It might be to improve your work-life balance by taking a big pay cut for a lower-stress role. It's OK to feel scared about the unknown. But as bestselling author Susan Jeffers says, you've got to feel the fear and do it anyway, otherwise nothing's going to change.

In 1998, three friends, Rich, Adam and Jon, were chatting on holiday and had the idea to start a business together. They decided to make some smoothies, buying £500 worth of fruit and selling them at the Jazz on the Green festival in Parsons Green, south-west London.

They put up a sign saying, 'Should we give up our jobs to make these smoothies?' In front of the stall were two bins: one labelled YES, one labelled NO. At the end of the day there were more empties in the YES bin. So they quit their jobs and started making smoothies for a living. And that's how the Innocent Drinks brand was born. Ten years later they sold a minority stake in the business to Coca-Cola for £30 million.

The Innocent founders gave up successful careers to take a punt on smoothies. But it fitted with their vision to start a business together. And their hard work paid off.

Let's start thinking about defining your vision. Think about why you bought this book, why you started on this journey. Remember that you wrote some notes towards the end of the second chapter: Taking Your First Steps (see page 38)? What did you say your dream job was? What did you say you wanted to get out of the programme?

THERE'S NEVER A BETTER TIME THAN NOW TO FOLLOW YOUR TRUE CALLING.

THE IDEA MINDSET

First, let's sketch out some initial thoughts in a vision statement. To make it memorable and effective, try to make your vision statement short, simple and precise. Make it specific and meaningful to you – if you read it back and think that it could describe just about anyone's dream working life, tweak it some more. And finally, it should be ambitious, exciting and achievable.

Just that.

I never said this was going to be easy!

YOUR VISION STATEMENT (INITIAL THOUGHTS):

....

....

....

....

....

Now you've got some initial thoughts down on paper, let's explore some choices to help you figure out the specifics of your future working life.

In the table below, tick the boxes that fit with where you see yourself. If neither of the options align with your goals, write some thoughts next to the questionnaire that more accurately reflect where you want to be.

	MOSTLY THIS	I DON'T MIND	MOSTLY THIS	
I never want to stop working				I want to retire early
I want to work full-time				I want to work part-time
I want to be rich				I'm happy if I'm just scraping by
I want to be famous				I want to be anonymous
I want to have power				I don't see power as a personal objective
I want to have influence				I'm not motivated by influencing others
I want to be the best in the country, or even the world, at what I do				I'm happy to be considered one of many people who is good at what they do
I see happiness as a goal				I don't see happiness as a goal in itself; it's an outcome of other goals
I prioritise money over happiness				I prioritise happiness over money
I prioritise money over power				I prioritise power over money
I prioritise power over happiness				I prioritise happiness over power
I prioritise satisfaction at home over satisfaction at work				I prioritise satisfaction at work over satisfaction at home
I want people to look to me				I want to stay in the background
I want to travel				I don't care about travelling
I want to see my partner or family every night				I'm happy to be away on business frequently

	MOSTLY THIS	I DON'T MIND	MOSTLY THIS	
I want to be part of something big				I don't care how big my goals are. If they impact just one person, that's good enough for me
I like being creative				I don't care about being creative
I want to leave a legacy				I'm not bothered about a legacy
I want to have one job				I want to have lots of different things going on at the same time
I want to be an expert				I want to know a little about lots of different things
I want to manage lots of people				I don't want to have to manage a team
I want to stay in the sector I work in today				I want to do something completely different
I expect to have to invest a lot of time, effort or money to get there				I've done enough paying out. Now I'm looking to be repaid for what I've already put in

Did this exercise help you understand what's important to you in your future working life? Was there anything here that you hadn't considered before?

Now let's refine your career vision statement. Is there anything you want to add in or take away, having answered these questions?

Think about what it would feel like to communicate your vision to someone else. Is it clear and easy to explain?

YOUR VISION STATEMENT (FINAL VERSION):

....

....

....

....

....

....

Exercise 2: Defining Your Purpose

Your purpose is why you get out of bed. It tends to be related to the broader positive societal impact you consider your work to have or would like it to have. It's the difference you're making every day.

For instance, that might be helping people to live longer, happier lives or access goods, services, treatment or advice which they would otherwise struggle to get hold of, thus facilitating social equality. It might be about connecting people or protecting the planet for future generations.

Your purpose might be something more focused on your immediate work environment – coming up with new, innovative ideas, helping your team develop and progress or delivering an amazing experience for your customers.

Whatever form it takes, it's about feeling a sense of **Engagement** and **Authenticity** in what you do. When people feel disengaged from their work or frustrated with colleagues, the issue is often that what they're doing with their time isn't aligned with their purpose.

When my great-aunt, a cleaner in the neonatal unit, was asked what she did for a living, she said, 'I look after the babies.' She kept the environment clean and infection-free, and when she plugged in her vacuum cleaner she took care to make sure she didn't unplug any of the incubators by accident. She saw her role in the context of helping the newborn babies to build up their strength in a clean and safe environment.

In their book *Will It Make the Boat Go Faster?*, authors Ben Hunt-Davis and Harriet Beveridge unpick the mentality of an Olympic rower and how a simple daily mission translates into the achievement of audacious performance goals – in Ben's case, winning Olympic Gold in the 2000 Sydney Olympic Games. This is a brilliant example of the essence of a compelling vision, purpose and goal. The vision – to win Olympic Gold – is inextricably tied into a clear purpose for each athlete individually and the team collectively to reach their full potential, test the limits of human capability and inspire others to do the same. The goal? To make the boat go faster.

What's your purpose? What gets you going every day? Write down your initial thoughts in a purpose statement below.

The way you describe your purpose should be simple, clear and inspiring. Think about what you'd like to say when someone asks you what you do for a living. Think about what would bring a smile to your face when talking about aspects of your future working life. What brings you joy and why?

NO ONE ELSE CAN TELL YOU WHAT YOU STAND FOR. NO ONE ELSE CAN DEFINE YOUR PURPOSE.

THE IDEA MINDSET

YOUR PURPOSE STATEMENT (INITIAL THOUGHTS):

....

....

....

....

....

Now answer the following questions to refine your thinking. Let's think about where you're at your best.

GIVE EXAMPLES OF HOW YOU APPLY
YOUR STRENGTHS AT WORK:

....

....

....

....

....

....

....

....

....

GIVE EXAMPLES OF RECENT WORK SUCCESSES:

....

....

....

....

....

....

....

....

....

....

GIVE EXAMPLES OF WAYS YOU CAN MAKE
A DIFFERENCE IN YOUR WORK:

....

....

....

....

....

LIST THREE PEOPLE WHO INSPIRE YOU IN YOUR WORK AND WHY:

....

....

....

....

....

Now, reflecting on these thoughts, re-articulate your purpose statement below.

YOUR PURPOSE STATEMENT (FINAL VERSION):

....

....

....

....

....

Exercise 3: Setting Your Goals

Now we're going to get into more of the detail: what your vision for your working life looks like in specific, real-world terms.

'Setting goals is the first step in turning the invisible into the visible.'

TONY ROBBINS, LIFE AND BUSINESS COACH

Why not jump straight to the action plan?

Often people get excited about their big career vision and move straight to their action plan. It *can* work, but there are trip hazards along the way because of the big-picture nature of your vision versus the detailed nature of your action plan. Your goals bridge the gap between the two. Being clear on your **Direction** in this way will feed your developing sense of **Engagement** and **Authenticity**.

Let's go back to the idea of building your house.

What's the vision? That's your dream home. What are your requirements? Maybe your dream home would be arranged in such a way that you could look out of the kitchen window at the children playing in the garden. Maybe you need a space where you could work from home without distractions. These requirements are just two of the components of your vision – your goals.

What's the action plan in this context? First, there are all the things that need to be done when you're constructing any kind of dwelling, regardless of whether it has a window out to the garden or not! For example, you're going to need to think about plumbing, heating and insulation.

Then you come to the detailed steps that, together, deliver the specific goals for your dream house: you need to ensure that at least one wall of the kitchen is parallel to the garden, for instance.

You might set a goal to have a cosy work den in the loft, away from the noise of the rest of the house. You google 'home office' and research some options, then make a neat, detailed 'home office action plan' of what you need and how you'll deliver it.

Think about the hundreds or thousands of individual steps required to build your dream home. Can you see how your action plan could get complicated and a bit out of control without the framework of your goals to guide you? It would be easy to forget something that you later realise you consider essential to your vision.

Your goals break down your career vision into manageable mini objectives.

How to write a goal

Before you make a start on writing your own goals, let's look at the following examples to guide you on how it's done:

Example 1 – simple:

- My vision is to set up my own personal-training business.
- My goals are:
    - to become a qualified personal trainer
    - to be a great business manager
    - to give back to the local community wherever I base my business

Example 2 – more specific:

- My vision is to step back to part-time work and spend more time with my growing family.
- My goals are:
    - to be working three and a half to four days per week
    - to earn a total annual income of £50,000
    - to have two week-long family holidays each year
    - to put my kids to bed every night
    - to have dinner with the family six nights a week and make dinner twice
    - to work from home one day per week

Remember that at this stage you are not yet writing an action plan. Instead, your goals should be the mini objectives that make up your vision. They each represent a *destination*, but not the method you use to get there. For example, 'have a clean kitchen' is a goal, but 'wash the dishes' is an action. Once you've achieved all your goals, your vision will have been realised.

Bear in mind that, once finalised, your goals should remain fairly constant, even if the set of specific actions that you need to carry out to deliver those goals – your action plan – needs to change according to circumstances.

Some examples of goals to get you thinking:

- To lead a team of three people.
- To be recognised as an expert in my chosen field by a trusted institution.
- To have my weekends back.
- To have twice the fun and half the stress.
- To be doing things that leave a legacy.
- To bring my idea to market and make my first £100,000 in sales.

Let's create some goals!

In the table below, write down some words or short phrases that you think could be part of your goals. Don't worry about putting these into complete sentences for now – what's important is to find the right words or phrases that express what's in your head. If you run out of space, write down more words or phrases on an extra sheet of paper.

WORD OR PHRASE	WHY IT'S IMPORTANT

Now, we're going to turn your long list into a short and focused set of goals.

Take the words (or phrases) from your list above and write each on a piece of paper or sticky note – one piece of paper for each word or phrase. Cluster together words or phrases that naturally fit together.

In the example below, see how the six words or phrases are grouped into three clusters, with each cluster representing a particular topic.

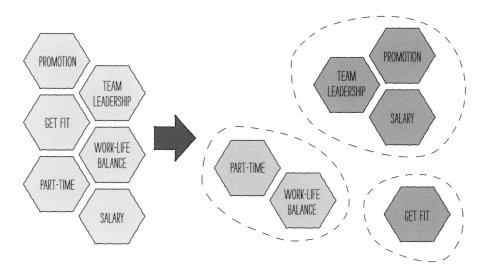

From these clusters, we can then build the words and phrases into goals. In this example, your goals might be:

1. Have a great work-life balance with part-time working.
2. Lead a team in a bigger role that earns a higher salary.
3. Get fit.

Once you're comfortable that you've got the goals right, think about the specific language you're going to use for each. Try to make the goals short and focused – resist the temptation to use a lot of words.

When you've done this, write your goals in the table below.

	GOALS
GOAL 1	
GOAL 2	
GOAL 3	
GOAL 4	
GOAL 5	
GOAL 6	

Now think about the order of your goals. They should follow some kind of logical flow. This could be:

- **Priorities** – Goal 1 is your most important area of focus
- **Dependencies** – you need to address Goal 1 to be able to achieve Goal 2
- **Story** – the number-one thing you want people to be aware of is Goal 1

How many goals should you have?

There is no hard and fast rule here, but three is probably too few and seven is probably too many. If you have more than six, see if you can consolidate two into one.

If you've got too many goals, it can feel a bit like a laundry list rather than the basis of a focused plan. A short, focused list of goals where you can spend quality time on each is better than a long and complicated list of goals where you're constantly flitting between different priorities.

Rewrite your goals here, with any adjustments you've made and in what you feel is the most logical order for you.

	GOALS
GOAL 1	
GOAL 2	
GOAL 3	
GOAL 4	
GOAL 5	
GOAL 6	

Getting your goals worded exactly right can be difficult, but it's worth investing time here because your goals are the framework for the changes you're going to make in your career and in your life. Once you've got your goals set out, everything else is much more likely to fall into place.

'Effort and courage are not enough without purpose and direction.'
JOHN F. KENNEDY

Power Move 1: Share Your Vision and Purpose

Find two or three people you trust and who know you well. They might be family members, close friends or trusted work colleagues. Take some time with them one day when you're relaxed and not overwhelmed or overworked. Talk about this journey you're on and how you're feeling about it. Explain your career vision and your purpose, and talk through why it's important to you. Ask them to share what they think about what you've said, then capture their words and phrases here.

FEEDBACK RECEIVED ON YOUR VISION AND PURPOSE:

After you've had these conversations, write some thoughts in your Reflective Journal (see page 86). How did it feel to share your vision and purpose? How did it feel to hear the feedback on it? What does that make you think about what you want to do next?

Power Move 2: Create Time to Think

We're still early in the programme. You're probably struggling to fit in this extra work alongside your everyday life. With the best will in the world, you might be getting to the end of the week and finding that you haven't done all the things you needed to do. Sadly, life isn't going to gift you some bonus hours in the day to fill in your Reflective Journal!

So you need a Power Move that creates time for you. Then you're going to use that time to do what you need to do to achieve your goals and reach your dream career. Many of my clients describe the IDEA Mindset as a feeling of having more time. Getting rid of self-doubt and regret means you spend more time thinking about how you want to spend your future.

Choose one or more of the three options below that are going to work best for you. Or why not give all three a whirl? You'll be amazed at the time you claw back.

Move A: Start a daily to-do list

This is for people who haven't got time because they're not organised in their everyday life. You react to what's happening and you don't plan ahead. You can feel as though you're drowning because new tasks are piling up more quickly than you can work through them. When you're overwhelmed by what you're dealing with already, it's almost impossible to add on anything new.

When you get up in the morning and are sitting with your morning coffee, grab a piece of paper and write down the things you have to do today. If you don't have to do it today, don't put it on the list. Stick the piece of paper in your pocket. Celebrate crossing off the items as you go through the day. Creating a to-do list is an easy way to give you focus and momentum, meaning you'll get through things faster because you'll be spending less time spinning round in circles, wondering what to tackle next or dealing with unimportant tasks. Ta-da – you've created some time!

Move B: Delegate

Lots of things you do can only be done by you. But think about whether there's one task, one job, one chore that you can delegate to someone else. Maybe it's a task at work that you can give to a junior team member as an opportunity to develop. Maybe you can get some more help at home to free up some time. We tend to hold onto doing tasks ourselves for a long time rather than letting them go. But that's time when we're not free to do other stuff, and that other stuff might be more important, more valuable, more uniquely dependent on our skills – like planning out your perfect working life. Only you can do that.

Find at least one thing in your life, ideally two, that you can hand over to someone else. A work task you can delegate to a team member. A household chore you can ask your partner to help with. Make it happen today. Free up some time.

YOU PLEDGE TO DELEGATE
(TASK)_____ TO (NAME)_____

....

....

....

....

....

Move C: Stop an activity

As a species we're generally great at starting things. We're pretty good at keeping going with things, too. We're not so good at letting things go. We don't like to stop things. 'I don't want to stop my project in case it finally comes good next week, despite years of failure.' 'I don't want to stop that big meeting because it makes people feel included, even though the content is not that valuable.'

Imagine you're trying to tidy your new shoes away in a cupboard, but the cupboard is already stuffed full of your old, worn-out shoes. For every pair of new shoes you want to put in the cupboard, you're going to have to take out a pair of your old, worn shoes. Otherwise you'll ruin the new shoes by trying to stuff them into the corner.

That's why it's important to stop things: you need to create space to start new things.

WE'RE GENERALLY BETTER AT STARTING THINGS THAN STOPPING THINGS. LEARN TO LET GO OF THE THINGS THAT FRUSTRATE YOU THE MOST OR SLOW YOU DOWN.

THE IDEA MINDSET

You can stop doing things (or reduce the time you're spending on them) in three ways:

1. You can stop the work from happening at all. That report you send out on a Friday which no one reads? Don't write it. Research by Webexpenses in 2019 found that the average worker spends two hours a day on pointless tasks – admin, manual paperwork and pointless meetings.[3]

2. You can reduce the amount of work involved in doing the work. Shorten the report. Send the report out every two weeks, or once a month, instead of every week. But only if people will read it when you do. Going to the supermarket every other day because you're missing something in the fridge? Plan ahead better so you have to go to the shop less frequently.

3. You can remove yourself from the conversation. If you don't need to be in the meeting, remove yourself from the invite. Or if you only need to be in part of it, tell the meeting chair in advance that you will only attend for the relevant part. Agree with your partner

that each of you can make certain decisions about your home life without the other one's explicit agreement. Set the parameters so you can get on and make decisions faster, with less time in the family committee.

Find one of these things, ideally two, that you can stop doing to free up a material amount of time.

YOU ARE GOING TO STOP ...

....

....

....

HOW DOES THIS GIVE YOU MORE TIME?

....

....

....

By the way, if you only write something here and you don't actually stop doing it, you've just undertaken another pointless task!

Whether enacted individually or together, Moves A, B and C will help you create more time to think.

Now, here's the magic. Don't let the space created by these moves get filled up by other things that just drop into the gap. Create the space, then shore it up with timber on each side. Protect the space. Block it out in your diary. Turn on your Out of Office. Turn off your phone or leave it in another room. Lock it in a safe. This is your time; care for it as you would a kitten, and use it wisely.

You're creating time – time that you will invest in shaping your perfect working life. And in that time your IDEA Mindset will emerge.

Week 2: Set the Course – Reflections

You've made it through Week 2 and built the foundations of your plan. Congratulations!

Like the guy ropes on a tent, the work you've done this week will anchor your action plan and provide stability. If you lose momentum or focus when you're in the detail, or you have to make a decision and you're not sure which path to take, you can always come back to your vision, purpose and goals to see the bigger picture. That's when you know that the work you've done this week is doing its job.

Your IDEA Mindset: self-reflection

As with Week 1, you're going to score yourself on how far you think you've moved forward on each of the IDEA Mindset components compared with where you were at the start of this week. Remember the definitions:

Identity

Clarity about who you are, what you stand for and the issues that are important to you. What your strengths are and the situations in which you excel. How others perceive you and whether that chimes with how you feel about yourself. A sense of self-assurance, an inner compass.

Direction

Clarity about the path ahead of you, what your long-term career goals are and knowing which way you'd turn when faced with a choice. Making forward progress along the path to your perfect career. A sense of comfort with the decisions you've made.

Engagement

Your level of connection with your life and work. How enthusiastic you are about the day ahead and how much of a sense of fulfilment you feel at the end of the day. You are excited about possible career opportunities ahead. Maybe you can see a path to a situation you'd love to be in.

Authenticity

Clarity about how your behaviour and choices at work connect with your values and sense of purpose. Your level of emotional connection with your life and work. Your passion. You're clear on why you're doing what you're doing, or, if not, you're starting to shape a path to an authentic future career.

Put a plus symbol in the appropriate box of the diagram below if you think you've moved forward on one or more of these IDEA Mindset components with the work you've done this week. Put more than one plus if you think you've moved forward a lot. Think about the way you've felt at work, and about the conversations you've had with friends and colleagues. Is your mindset changing?

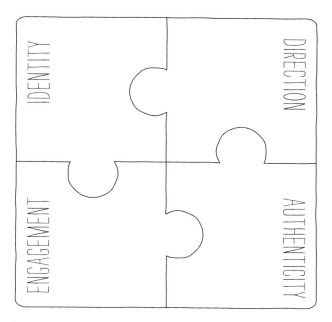

Remember to write some notes in your Reflective Journal (see page 86). Write about how you found this week and if there's anything that you notice is changing in your life and work as you continue on this journey.

Accountability Memo

You're already starting to put new actions in place – new regular habits, new routines, new behaviours. Use this Accountability Memo to capture a list of all the things you're doing today which you weren't doing when you started reading the book. It'll help you to keep hold of those new actions and stay accountable.

....

....

....

....

....

....

....

....

....

....

....

....

....

TAKEAWAY THOUGHT: It usually takes time to find the perfect words to articulate what's in your head. Give yourself permission to come back and tweak the words you've written in the exercises each week as you reflect on them and evolve your thinking. That's part of the process of finding clarity.

WEEK 3

PREPARE YOUR MIND AND BODY FOR CHANGE

To change your life and fulfil your career dreams, you're going to need mental resilience. Resilience is a big part of your IDEA Mindset. Are you ready to take action? Are you empowered to make change happen? Do you feel energised? When you need to, can you cope under pressure?

You need a clear head and a healthy body to realise your full potential at work. We're not talking about running marathons here – everyone's different. You'll know what you want to achieve to set yourself up for the future.

Mental health and wellness have never been as high on the agenda as they are now. The prevalence of mental health issues, and the positive impact that mental resilience can have on our happiness and ability to cope in difficult situations, are being recognised now more than ever.

Taking the first step is hard enough, but delivering on all your career goals requires commitment, motivation, perseverance and resilience. You're on a difficult and challenging journey, with plenty of uncertainty ahead and bends in the road to navigate. You need to be firing on all cylinders mentally to help you achieve your goals, even on a day when you're not feeling it.

'We're facing a stress and burnout epidemic. And ... people deeply want to change the way they work and live.'
ARIANNA HUFFINGTON,
AUTHOR AND
BUSINESSWOMAN

When Mildred and I were training for a big competition, we would be in the studio almost every night. Some days we felt inspired and motivated. Other days not so much. Maybe we'd had a bad day at work. Often we had residual aches and pains from a hard training session earlier in the week. Sometimes things just didn't connect in the dance – our bodies didn't coordinate perfectly as we needed them to for efficient movement around the floor. For years we struggled with how to process this feeling of not being able to deliver our best performance in each training session.

One day our coach said to us, 'You don't have to achieve your best performance. Just come to the training session with one clear goal and deliver that. It might be to perfect a specific technical move. It might be to move as far as you possibly can across the floor. It might be to fill the largest volume of space with your two bodies. Find that micro-goal and let go of everything else.'

It transformed our mindset and gave us resilience to deal with the difficult times. We delivered more in total by focusing on individual elements and letting go of the need to be perfect every time.

Today, when I'm coaching a client, there are always lots of things I think I can be doing better. Noticing my client's emotional responses, creating more silence for them to think in, asking more thoughtful questions that take them into areas of new insight. At the start of each coaching session I pick one area that I'm going to focus on developing. I'm aiming to continually improve how I can serve my clients, but I don't beat myself up for not being perfect.

By working on your mental wellbeing and resilience, you're setting yourself up to reach your career goals and, crucially, make the changes stick.

There are three exercises you're going to complete this week.

We'll start with a **Resilience Self-assessment** (see page 141), which will reveal how resilient you really are and show how you can strengthen your resilience.

Next, we'll move on to a **Sleep Diary** (see page 148). Getting the right amount of good-quality sleep is very important if we want to refresh and recharge.

> 'Some days there won't be a song in your heart. Sing anyway.'
> **EMORY AUSTIN, MOTIVATIONAL SPEAKER AND BREAST CANCER SURVIVOR**

Finally, we're going to complete a **Diet and Fitness Diary** (see page 154). Physical wellness gives you the energy you need to make change happen and is a powerful enabler of mental resilience.

This week your two Power Moves are:

1. Positivity Push (see page 164)
2. Write Your Affirmation (see page 166)

 SOUNDTRACK TO YOUR WEEK

This week's soundtrack is about resilience and empowerment.

Play this track before you start the week's reading and exercises to get you in the mood: 'Fire and Rain' by James Taylor. Watch the live version recorded at the Colonial Theatre in 2007, where you can pick up his every emotion as he performs the song.

Play this track on repeat in the background when you're doing your reading, thinking and writing: *Trois Gymnopédies* by Erik Satie. These calming, meditative pieces for piano written in the late 1880s will help you centre your thoughts and calm your mind. Claude Debussy's *Clair de Lune* has a similar effect.

Play this track when you're done, in a celebration of completion and to provide the uplifting energy you need to move on to the next step: 'SHUT UP + DANCE' by Walk the Moon. This 2014 hit gives you a change in pace and energy as you build towards the next step in your plan. It's about letting go and having fun!

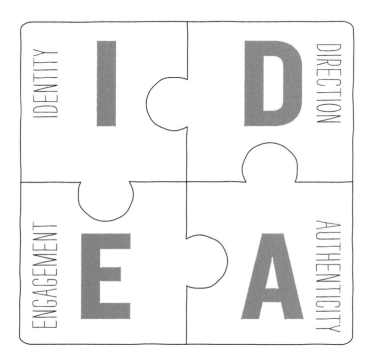

The Route to Gold

Katarina Johnson-Thompson is a world-champion British heptathlete. She was recognised from a young age as one of the brightest young British athletic talents of her generation, but her journey to becoming world champion was exceptionally difficult. Having arrived on the scene with a strong performance at the

London 2012 Olympics, she promised much over the next few years but failed to deliver on the biggest stages.

In 2015, at the World Athletics Championships in Beijing, she was strongly placed to challenge for Gold after the first day of events and then committed three fouls in the long jump, dropping completely out of contention. For a year afterwards, she set the image of her foot overstepping the long jump board as the screensaver on her laptop.

At the Rio Olympics in 2016, poor performances in the shot-put and javelin events again left her outside of the medals. Reflecting afterwards, she said, '[The throwing events] are just weaknesses. Everybody is constantly talking to me about it. It doesn't help.' Even her coach thought she should try a different event.

In December 2016, Johnson-Thompson decided to change her life. Leaving her native Liverpool behind, she switched coaches and moved her life and belongings to a small apartment in Montpellier in the South of France. 'It's been a complete life overhaul. In Liverpool I was very settled … Here, everyone speaks a different language.' She credited the move with a change in her mental resilience. 'Psychologically, I was in a bad place last year … I just didn't want to train. I didn't want to compete in case I got injured.' Her new French coaches nicknamed her 'Droopy' due to her downbeat demeanour when she first arrived. 'I sort of didn't enjoy anything over the last two years … I set high expectations for myself and when I didn't reach those expectations it was hard for me to face.'

However, isolating herself from the pressures that had plagued her in recent years began to reap rewards. Her coaches created a more relaxed environment in which to train and she learned to be less dependent on others. 'Out here, I am doing literally everything myself … I am a proper adult now, I think.' Gradually, step by step, she built her confidence and improved her ability to string together a series of world-class performances without a stumble.

It didn't happen straight away. At the World Championships in London in 2017, a weaker-than-expected performance in the high jump cost her a medal and she finished in fifth place. 'I hit a real low with that performance. But it was a stupid one-off high jump where my ankles felt really bad in the rain. It really affected me mentally and I was wrong to let it get to me ... It taught me that you have to be in the moment, and you can't allow one little thing to stop you. I needed to be mentally tougher.'

With time came results. As the 2019 World Championships came around, Johnson-Thompson reflected on her improved preparation in Montpellier. 'At the last Worlds I was only a summer into my move to France and ... I wasn't settled in the slightest. I also didn't have any belief in myself ... but it seems like a lifetime ago now.' Breaking her personal best in the 100 metres and matching her biggest rival in the high jump, Johnson-Thompson faced the shot-put – the source of many of her previous failures. Her throw of 13.86 metres was 71 centimetres further than she had ever thrown before. She held the lead at the end of day one. In her second throwing event, the javelin – again a major weakness in her previous performances – she threw another personal best of 43.93 metres. She went into the final event in Gold Medal position, ahead of the reigning Olympic Champion.

As the biggest moment of her sporting career approached, she was ready as she stood on the 800 metres start line. 'I certainly don't take anything for granted with my past history, but I was so up for it ... literally, this is the moment.' Another personal best confirmed both World Championship Gold and the British record. Completing her lap of honour, she reflected on her journey. 'I can't believe this is the result ... The low moments have helped me come back and make the move [to Montpellier] and try to look inward on myself.'

Later, Johnson-Thompson reflected on her mental resilience. 'Being labelled world champion has an authority to it. But it's weird to me because I feel like the same person, with the same emotions, doubts and fears. Now I look at other [previous world champions] and think they must have been scared at certain points, too, but I didn't think it at the time because they had the label. Everyone is human, everyone has fears and anxieties and makes mistakes. I was just lucky that in that competition I had learned to use them in certain ways and block them out in certain ways.'

Johnson-Thompson's road to the top was personally crafted, with passion, commitment and drive, against all the odds. Taking deliberate and mindful steps to build her mental resilience, to maximise her talent and strengths, she was able to finally fulfil her extraordinary potential. It was not luck. 'It's actually helped knowing that I have experienced that low and that I am OK now ... those performances don't represent me as a person, [they don't] make me a bad person. I've got myself a little life. I moved to France. I just sorted through my life.'[4]

What Is Mental Resilience?

Simply put, mental resilience is about being able to cope under pressure. If you're accelerating, if you're changing direction or if you're struggling against a headwind, you're under pressure. If you're a high achiever, then you might have created a lot of that pressure for yourself!

There are six levers that can help you build stronger mental resilience – what I call the 'Six Ps': Positivity, Problem-solving, Perspective, Personality, Persistence and Partnering.

Positivity

Positivity is about having a positive mental attitude and a positive relationship with others. By focusing on what we can change – our attitude, and how we behave towards and around other people – and letting go of what is out of our control, we can put our energy to the best possible use. Of course, life isn't always about sunshine and rainbows, but look for the times when you have control over the narrative and make sure your self-talk and interactions are positive.

Remember when we talked about how your internal narrative can change from 'Why haven't you …?' or 'Why didn't you …?' to something more uplifting (see page 30)? Try flipping negative thoughts on their head for a positive spin, like this:

'Imagine if I just …!'

'I wonder if I could …!'

'What if I …?'

'What if we …?'

> 'The past does not equal the future unless you live there.'
>
> TONY ROBBINS, AUTHOR AND COACH

Problem-solving

Problem-solving is about shifting from a 'problem mindset' to a 'solution mindset'. Think about the times when things have been tough and all you could do was rage and grumble about how awful everything was, how it was broken, how it was someone else's fault, how mad you were about the whole situation. When those moments arise in the future, think about how you might be able to turn your inner thoughts to what you can do to make a difference, to improve the situation and to find a solution.

What's a common source of frustration for you that you could reframe more positively?

Example: 'The people I work with are so frustrating. My plan is obviously the right way forward and they don't get it. We need to get on with it …' becomes … 'I think I need to work harder on explaining my thinking to my colleagues. It's helpful sometimes when they make me slow down and consider the options more carefully.'

What's an example of a situation in the past when you didn't think you were going to be able to succeed but you found a way through? What was the moment when you worked out how to move forward? What did *you* do?

'Every lock has a key.'

VARIOUS

Perspective

How many times recently have you become frustrated at something that wasn't actually that big a deal? Having a short fuse when you're stressed and tired means it doesn't take much to send you over the edge.

From time to time, carve out a little time in your diary and go out for a walk somewhere you like that inspires you. For the duration of that walk, park all the stressful stuff you're dealing with and look to the future. Imagine your life in a few months or a year's time, when you're further along the path to your ideal work set-up. What are you looking forward to? What's going to feel different?

When you get back from your walk, grab a piece of paper and write down two or three phrases that encapsulate your hopes for the future. Put that piece of paper in an envelope and store it in your bedside table or your desk, so you can check back on it when everything's getting on top of you.

'There are always flowers for those who want to see them.'

HENRI MATISSE

Personality

You have to know yourself to build your mental resilience. Every day, work on bringing your awareness to how you're thinking and feeling, particularly in moments of intensity. Notice how your manner and behaviour shifts, and how your body responds physically to differ-

> 'Learn to know yourself ... to search realistically and regularly the processes of your own mind and feelings.'
>
> NELSON MANDELA

ent situations. Understand what triggers you. Try to think about the first thing that sets you off.

Reflect on the environment you're in when it happens. What happened before to make you react in this way today? What else is going on for you today? The better you know yourself, the better you're able to first pre-empt, then control your emotions and behaviours in challenging situations. This is a powerful skill and it's at the heart of the IDEA Mindset.

Persistence

Making change happen is tough. Sometimes things don't go your way. It's important not to get blown off course by the first sign of crosswinds. Persistence helps you to keep pushing for the summit even when it's hard. You get better at it with practice. Long-distance runners talk about practising spending time close to their physical limit so that it becomes familiar and not a feeling that makes them quit.

> 'We do not need magic to transform our world. We carry all the power we need inside ourselves already.'
>
> J.K. ROWLING

On the other hand, you also need to recognise your limits. If you're finding that you're struggling and can't see a way out (either of a specific situation or a negative headspace), or you're in over your head, don't ignore it. Stop, take a breath, ask for help.

The long-distance runner will stop if there's a risk of a significant injury.

Think of a time recently when you *almost* gave up. What caused you to falter? What helped you keep going?

Partnering

Partnering is about having a great support network around you. They might be your friends, your family, a mentor or a coach. Who are the people you turn to when you need advice or support? Who are the people who help you feel comfortable and confident in the decisions you make?

When you're dealing with a challenge at work, who do you chat through the problem with?

When something's getting you down, who do you call on? Who *could* you call on that you might not have considered?

If mental health and resilience is a particular challenge for you, or if you would just like to explore this area in more detail, you should contact a qualified health professional. I have also recommended some further reading at the end of this book (see pages 288–90).

> 'No one can whistle a symphony. It takes a whole orchestra to play it.'
>
> H.E. LUCCOCK,
> METHODIST MINISTER

Exercise 1: Resilience Self-assessment

Let's complete an exercise exploring how you can strengthen your resilience using each of the Six Ps.

With the scoring, remember that moving from a 2 to a 3 is just as good as moving from an 8 to a 9. It's all about forward momentum. One step at a time.

POSITIVITY

'I am a fairly upbeat person who generally sees life positively and optimistically. When faced with a challenging situation, I usually find something positive and build on that.'

On a scale of 1 to 10, how true is this statement?

....

Is this higher or lower than where you were one year ago?

....

One thing you could do differently to improve this score by 1 point:

....

....

....

....

PROBLEM-SOLVING

'I don't think I'm a natural grumbler. When faced with a challenging situation, I switch my thinking quickly to what can be done about it.'

On a scale of 1 to 10, how true is this statement?

....

Is this higher or lower than where you were one year ago?

....

One thing you could do differently to improve this score by 1 point:

....

....

....

....

....

PERSPECTIVE

'I think of myself as a fairly level-headed person. When faced with a challenging situation, I'm good at keeping things in perspective.'

On a scale of 1 to 10, how true is this statement?

....

Is this higher or lower than where you were one year ago?

....

One thing you could do differently to improve this score by 1 point:

....

....

....

....

PERSONALITY

'I rarely let my emotions get the better of me. When faced with a challenging situation, I am conscious of my thoughts and emotions — what they are, how and why they come about — and, as a result, I understand how to bring them under control.'

On a scale of 1 to 10, how true is this statement?

....

Is this higher or lower than where you were one year ago?

....

One thing you could do differently to improve this score by 1 point:

....

....

....

....

....

PERSISTENCE

'I am persistent, but I also know my limits. When faced with a challenging situation, I keep going even when it's tough, but I also know when to take a break.'

On a scale of 1 to 10, how true is this statement?

....

Is this higher or lower than where you were one year ago?

....

One thing you could do differently to improve this score by 1 point:

....

....

....

....

....

PARTNERING

> 'I am confident of my own abilities, but I know when to seek help, and where to go when I need it.'

On a scale of 1 to 10, how true is this statement?

....

Is this higher or lower than where you were one year ago?

....

One thing you could do differently to improve this score by 1 point:

....

....

....

....

....

ONE THING I LEARNED FROM DOING THIS EXERCISE:

....

....

....

....

....

Exercise 2: Sleep Diary

Sleep is important for both mental health and physical wellbeing, but different people need different amounts of sleep. The NHS recommends between six and nine hours for most adults.[5]

Most of us know that not getting enough sleep can leave us feeling grumpy, irritable and unable to work at our best. But lack of sleep is also a risk factor for obesity, heart disease and diabetes, and has been connected to shortened life expectancy. People who are sleep-deprived have reduced levels of leptin (the hormone that makes us feel full) and increased levels of ghrelin (the hormone that makes us feel hungry).[6]

Arianna Huffington, co-founder of the Huffington Post and CEO of Thrive Global, is now an advocate of the power of sleep wellness in reducing the risk of burnout. Her passion is driven by her own experience of burnout, in which she fainted from sleep deprivation and exhaustion, hit her head on her desk and broke her cheekbone.

In this exercise you will complete a sleep diary for the next seven days. This will help you to be more aware of your own sleep patterns and the factors that influence whether or not you get a good night's sleep. Try to do the sleep diary in a 'normal' week that represents your usual level of activity (and stress!), so not when you are on holiday or doing a major one-off project. This sleep diary should represent your everyday life. But before you start, answer the questions below.

'If we're going to truly thrive, we must begin with sleep. It's the gateway through which a life of wellbeing must travel.'
ARIANNA HUFFINGTON, AUTHOR AND BUSINESSWOMAN

DO YOU CONSIDER YOURSELF A GOOD SLEEPER? WHY?

....

....

....

HOW MANY HOURS OF SLEEP DO YOU THINK
YOU GET ON AVERAGE A NIGHT? HOW MANY DO
YOU NEED TO PERFORM AT YOUR BEST?

....

....

....

WHAT STOPS YOU GETTING MORE AND BETTER SLEEP?

....

....

....

Now it's time to complete a sleep diary. For the next seven days, track your sleep behaviours in the following table, using a notebook or a separate sheet of paper if you need. Try not to move too far away from your normal sleep pattern just because you're doing the exercise.

	DAY 1	DAY 2	DAY 3	DAY 4	DAY 5	DAY 6	DAY 7
Day of the week							
Time you woke up this morning							
Three words for how you felt when you woke up this morning							
Three things you did in the hour before you went to bed last night							
Time spent getting to sleep last night							
Time spent asleep last night							
Did you wake up during the night?							
Three words for your mood through the day today							
Average stress level through the day today, from 1 (low stress) to 10 (high stress)							
How many caffeinated drinks did you consume today?							
How many minutes of exercise did you do today?							
Did you have a nap during the day?							

Once you have completed your sleep diary, answer the following questions.

> ## WERE YOU SURPRISED WHEN YOU COMPARED YOUR EXPECTATIONS WITH REALITY?
>
> ....
>
> ....
>
> ....

> ## WHAT THINGS SEEMED TO BE ASSOCIATED WITH SLEEPING BETTER?
>
> ....
>
> ....
>
> ....

WHAT THINGS SEEMED TO BE ASSOCIATED
WITH SLEEPING LESS WELL?

....

....

....

IF YOU WERE TO DO ONE THING TO IMPROVE YOUR
QUALITY OF SLEEP, WHAT WOULD IT BE?

....

....

....

LIST THREE CHANGES YOU WILL MAKE TO YOUR SLEEPING ENVIRONMENT TO MARK YOUR COMMITMENT TO GETTING BETTER SLEEP:

1. ....

....

2. ....

....

3. ....

....

When you come to create your action plan next week, reflect on how you want to turn this intention into action.

Exercise 3: Diet and Fitness Diary

We're now going to look at how physical wellness readies you for change.

Physical wellness is about looking after our bodies to support optimal health and function. We're not talking about doing an Ironman challenge or finding your six-pack here – although if that's part of your goal, go for it! You're on a journey of change and you want to make sure the vehicle you're travelling in is up to the journey – tyres pumped up, oil level checked, exterior surfaces polished and a warning triangle in the boot in case of emergencies!

'Take care of your body. It's the only place you have to live.'

JIM ROHN,
MOTIVATIONAL
SPEAKER

Diet

Who you are and what you eat are inextricably linked. Your diet reflects your preferences, your beliefs, your upbringing, your mood, your health status, your financial situation, your goals. Whether omnivorous, pescatarian, vegetarian, vegan or flexitarian, all healthy diets have certain common characteristics, and they don't have to be expensive.

The NHS recommends that adults eat a balanced diet of:

- At least five portions of a variety of fruit and vegetables every day
- Meals based on higher-fibre starchy foods like potatoes, bread, rice or pasta
- Some dairy, or dairy alternatives
- Some protein – that can be fish, eggs or meat if you eat animal products, or it could be beans, pulses, tofu, quinoa, nuts or seeds if you don't
- Unsaturated oils and spreads, in small amounts
- Plenty of fluids – at least six to eight glasses a day

You should try to reduce your intake of food and drink which is high in fat, salt and sugar, and eat a sufficient amount to maintain your weight at a healthy level, as measured by your body mass index (BMI). Most people eat too many calories, too much saturated fat and too much sugar and salt – and not enough fruit, vegetables, oily fish and fibre.[7]

If you drink alcohol, you will avoid major health risks by keeping your weekly intake under control. You should also avoid individual heavy drinking sessions and aim to have several alcohol-free days each week. Guidance varies by country, so if you're not based in the UK do check local health guidelines.

It's common to underestimate your alcohol intake or actively stretch the truth when asked directly about it by doctors, so be honest with yourself – this is just for you.

Let's spend some time thinking about your diet.

WHAT DO YOU THINK YOU SHOULD EAT MORE OF?

....

....

....

WHAT DO YOU THINK YOU SHOULD EAT LESS OF?

....

....

....

HOW WOULD YOU DESCRIBE YOUR ALCOHOL INTAKE?

....

....

....

FACTORS THAT GET IN THE WAY OF YOU EATING
(AND DRINKING) A HEALTHY DIET:

....

....

....

Now it's time to complete a food and drink diary. There are a lot of apps out there to help you do this, which will also log your calorie intake and alcohol units. A couple of good ones are:

- MyFitnessPal
- Drinkaware

For the next seven days, track what you eat and drink in the following table. Feel free to use a notebook or a separate sheet of paper to do this, if you wish. Try not to move too far away from what you normally have just because you're doing the exercise.

	DAY 1	DAY 2	DAY 3	DAY 4	DAY 5	DAY 6	DAY 7
Day of the week							
Breakfast							
Lunch							
Dinner							
Snacks							
Non-alcoholic drinks							
Alcoholic drinks							
Units of alcohol consumed							
Did I plan to eat more healthily or drink less when I woke up this morning?							
If I didn't achieve my goal, what got in the way?							
Was this a normal day in terms of what I ate and drank?							

Now answer the following questions:

WHAT (IF ANYTHING) SURPRISED YOU ON COMPLETING THIS DIARY?

....

....

....

IDENTIFY ONE ASPECT OF YOUR DIET YOU'D LIKE TO CHANGE:

....

....

....

When you come to create your action plan next week, reflect on how you want to turn this intention into action.

Fitness

Want to reduce your risk of heart disease, stroke, type 2 diabetes and cancer by up to 50 per cent, lower your risk of early death by up to 30 per cent, boost your self-esteem, your mood, sleep quality and energy, *and* reduce your risk of stress, depression, dementia and Alzheimer's disease? It's all about achieving a better level of fitness.[8]

The NHS recommends at least 150 minutes a week of moderate-intensity exercise, or 75 minutes a week of vigorous exercise for 19–64-year-olds.[9] Moderate exercise might be, for example, brisk walking, cycling, dancing or hiking. Vigorous exercise could include jogging or running, swimming or cycling fast, playing sport or walking up hills.

If, after this week, you're hoping to increase the amount of exercise you do, it's important to build up gradually to minimise the risk of injury, particularly if you're starting from scratch, are a bit older, have been injured in the past or have other underlying health conditions. A good rule of thumb is to increase your exercise level no more than 10–15 per cent each week from what you did the week before.[10] If you have any concerns, you should seek the advice of a qualified health professional before starting an exercise programme.

Before completing your fitness diary, answer the preparatory questions below to get you started.

WHAT IS YOUR FAVOURITE FITNESS ACTIVITY AND WHY?

....

....

....

LIST THE FACTORS THAT HELP YOU TO STAY ACTIVE:

....

....

....

LIST THE FACTORS THAT GET IN THE WAY OF STAYING ACTIVE:

....

....

....

WHO DO YOU NEED ON YOUR TEAM TO HELP
YOU GET ENOUGH EXERCISE EACH WEEK?

....

....

....

Now complete a fitness diary for the week in the table below. Use a notebook or a separate sheet of paper to do this, if you need. Choose a week that is as typical of your normal life as possible, when you have your usual stresses and strains. The object here is to understand what you usually have time to do.

	DAY 1	DAY 2	DAY 3	DAY 4	DAY 5	DAY 6	DAY 7
Day of the week							
What type of exercise did I do today?							
How many minutes?							
What level of activity (moderate, vigorous)?							
Did I plan to do more when I woke up this morning?							
If I didn't achieve my goal, what got in the way?							
Was this a normal day in terms of the exercise I did?							

Now answer the following questions:

WHAT (IF ANYTHING) SURPRISED YOU ON COMPLETING THIS DIARY?

....

....

....

NAME ONE ASPECT OF YOUR FITNESS
REGIME YOU'D LIKE TO CHANGE:

....

....

....

When you come to create your action plan next week, reflect on how you want to turn this intention into action.

Power Move 1: Positivity Push

We talked earlier about the roles of positivity and perspective (two of the Six Ps) in building your mental resilience (see page 137). In this Power Move, you're going to look at your natural responses to negative situations and find ways to reframe them in a positive light. Below are some examples of immediate responses and how they might be reframed:

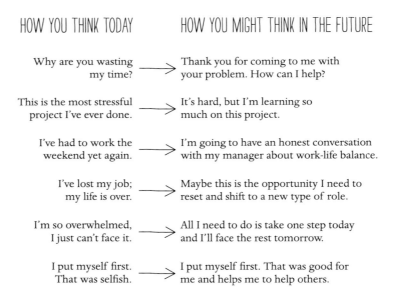

HOW YOU THINK TODAY | HOW YOU MIGHT THINK IN THE FUTURE

Why are you wasting my time? → Thank you for coming to me with your problem. How can I help?

This is the most stressful project I've ever done. → It's hard, but I'm learning so much on this project.

I've had to work the weekend yet again. → I'm going to have an honest conversation with my manager about work-life balance.

I've lost my job; my life is over. → Maybe this is the opportunity I need to reset and shift to a new type of role.

I'm so overwhelmed, I just can't face it. → All I need to do is take one step today and I'll face the rest tomorrow.

I put myself first. That was selfish. → I put myself first. That was good for me and helps me to help others.

Think of a time recently when you were extremely frustrated by something that happened, something someone said or something someone did. What was the situation and what was your immediate, instinctive response? What was the voice in your head saying? Write your answers below.

THE SITUATION:

....

....

....

WHAT THE VOICE IN YOUR HEAD WAS SAYING:

....

....

....

Now think about how you can frame that response in a more positive light.

WHAT'S A MORE POSITIVE FRAMING OF THAT RESPONSE?

....

....

....

Over the next few days I want you to notice those moments when that voice pipes up and your instinctive response is negative. Noticing the voice is the first step in making a change. Practise turning that negative into a more positive thought.

Power Move 2: Write Your Affirmation

Many people find that writing and repeating a simple affirmative phrase helps them to focus on a positive mindset when they're struggling. An affirmation is a very personal thing, but some examples to get you thinking are:

'I am enough.'

'I choose happiness.'

'The rest of my life is just beginning.'

'After the dark the sun always rises.'

'I am resourceful, I choose my path, I create my future.'

Use language that is personal to you to write your affirmation. Reflect on a compliment that meant a lot to you. Think about a persistent fear you have – what language might you use to dispel it? Think of a moment when you felt you were coming out of a dark time – what carried you through? Has anyone ever said something to you so meaningful that you wrote it down to reflect on later?

Write your personal affirmation below, and whenever you are in need of inspiration, close your eyes, slow your breathing and repeat it to yourself. Bring yourself back to that moment and reconnect with a feeling of positivity.

YOUR PERSONAL AFFIRMATION:

....

....

....

Now think about how you can make your affirmation more powerful. Think about the times in your life when you might want to remember it. Where and when does it need to show up? Could it pop up as a calendar reminder on your computer every morning? Perhaps you could set it as the wallpaper on your phone. Or it could be a Post-it note next to the chocolate stash!

HOW ARE YOU GOING TO BRING YOUR AFFIRMATION TO LIFE?

....

....

....

Week 3: Prepare Your Mind and Body for Change – Reflections

Congratulations on coming out the other side of Week 3!

Some of the issues we've talked about this week you might have been aware of already; others you might not really have thought about before. Some might be things you're comfortable talking about with family and friends; others might feel so personal or raw that you just want to keep them to yourself, at least for now. That's fine. This is your journey, and you need to find the approach that works for you.

Remember that the most successful people in the world are tripped up by a (very human) lack of resilience and it's not something you 'achieve' overnight, in a week, in a month or even in a year. Rather, it's a quality you continue to develop, and looking after your body and mind is integral to that process. Shifting your mindset takes time, and to do it you need to feel energised, motivated and strong, both physically and mentally.

If you do feel very sad, overwhelmed or angry tackling this week's exercises, or if the work you've done has made you realise that some of your behaviours could be problematic, you should reach out to a qualified health professional.

Your IDEA Mindset: self-reflection

As with Weeks 1 and 2, you're going to score yourself on how far you think you've moved forward on each of the IDEA Mindset components compared with where you were at the start of this week. Remember the definitions:

Identity

Clarity about who you are, what you stand for and the issues that are important to you. What your strengths are and the situations in which you excel. How others perceive you and whether that chimes with how you feel about yourself. A sense of self-assurance, an inner compass.

Direction

Clarity about the path ahead of you, what your long-term career goals are and knowing which way you'd turn when faced with a choice. Making forward progress along the path to your perfect career. A sense of comfort with the decisions you've made.

Engagement

Your level of connection with your life and work. How enthusiastic you are about the day ahead and how much of a sense of fulfilment you feel at the end of the day. You are excited about possible career opportunities ahead. Maybe you can see a path to a situation you'd love to be in.

Authenticity

Clarity about how your behaviour and choices at work connect with your values and sense of purpose. Your level of emotional connection with your life and work. Your passion. You're clear on why you're doing what you're doing, or, if not, you're starting to shape a path to an authentic future career.

Put a plus symbol in the appropriate box of the diagram below if you think you've moved forward on one or more of these IDEA Mindset components with the work you've done this week. Put more than one plus if you think you've moved forward a lot. Think about the way you've felt at work, and about the conversations you've had with friends and colleagues. Do you think your mindset is changing?

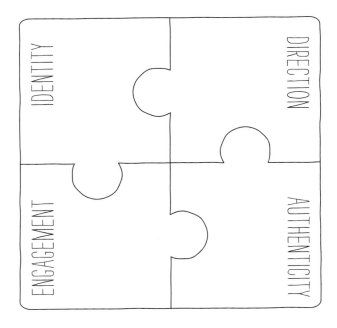

Remember to write some notes in your Reflective Journal (see page 86). Write about how you found this week and if there's anything that you notice is changing in your life and work as you continue on this journey.

Accountability Memo

You're continuing to put new actions in place – new regular habits, new routines, new behaviours. Use this Accountability Memo to capture a list of all the things you're doing today that you weren't doing when you started reading the book. It'll help you to keep hold of those new actions and to stay accountable.

....

....

....

....

....

....

....

....

....

....

....

....

....

TAKEAWAY THOUGHT: Building resilience can take a long time. Don't rush it and don't beat yourself up if it takes a while to make progress. Give it time, keep plugging away and you'll find what works for you.

WEEK 4

YOUR ACTION PLAN

Y ou're halfway through already. Three weeks down, three to go!

This is where we get to the good stuff, the juicy stuff, and we start turning all that great thinking into some powerful and impactful *doing*. This week you're going to intentionally create your future relationship with work. The kind of work that'll feel like you're doing exactly what you're meant to be doing, that plays to your strengths and gives you what you need for the life you want. Imagine what that will feel like!

This week we're thinking: what are you going to do to access your perfect work situation and unlock your IDEA Mindset, using all four of the tenets that by now you are developing? *How* are you going to do it? *Who* is going to help you? *When* are you going to do it by?

'A plan without action is not a plan. It's a speech.'

T. BOONE PICKENS, FINANCIER AND PHILANTHROPIST

There are three exercises you're going to complete this week.

First, we're **Creating Your Actions** (see page 182) – the individual steps you need to take in order to achieve your career goals.

Next, we'll move on to **Asking for Help** (see page 189), where you're going to think about who you need support from in completing your actions.

Finally, you're going to turn a list of actions into an achievable **Action Timeline** (see page 196).

This week your two Power Moves are:

1. Create the Calendar (see page 204)
2. Make an Irreversible Commitment (see page 204)

SOUNDTRACK TO YOUR WEEK

This week's soundtrack is about taking action and moving forward.

Play this track before you start the week's reading and exercises to get you in the mood: '*Chevaliers de Sangreal*' by Hans Zimmer. This powerful piece features in the film soundtrack for *The Da Vinci Code* from 2006 and represents an unrelenting, rhythmic crescendo driving the listener forward step by step. Check out the version Zimmer and his orchestra played in his live concert from Prague in May 2016.

Play this track on repeat in the background when you're doing your reading, thinking and writing: '**Moving**' by Secret Garden. Taken from the album *White Stones*, this track by the Norwegian duo Secret Garden embodies the energy of movement and forward progress. Watch the live version recorded in Kilden in 2015, and if you enjoy this piece then look up 'Windancer'.

Play this track when you're done, in celebration of completion and to provide the uplifting energy you need to move on to the next step: '**I'm Here**' by Cynthia Erivo. This iconic song from the Broadway musical *The Color Purple* captures an inspirational spirit of self-worth and ownership. Find the raw and heartfelt version recorded on *The Late Show with Stephen Colbert* in 2016.

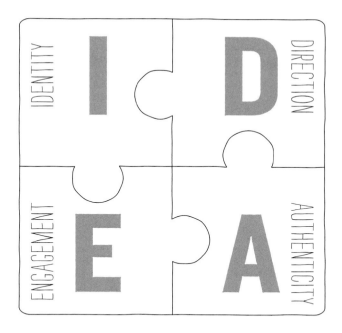

What Makes a Good Action Plan?

Your action plan is a list of the things you will do, who will do them and when they will be done. It needs to be clear and focused, and ambitious while also being achievable.

A great action plan looks simple but is quite hard to pull together – and that's before you've even started doing it! When it really works, it has levels of detail that you can unpeel like an onion.

In your action plan you're going to create a list of things you need to do to deliver your career goals as well as consider what help you'll need and your deadlines. The more you can think and plan through this detail, the less likely you are to be tripped up by something unexpected as you work through your action plan.

Life is rarely perfect and things don't always happen the way we predict, so a great action plan also requires anticipation and adaptability: anticipation of what's around the corner which you might need to prepare for; adaptability so you can adjust (or sometimes completely change) your plans if circumstances dictate. Many an action plan has failed because people have stuck rigidly to it without stepping back from time to time and thinking about whether they were still pursuing the best course of action.

When designing and running your action plan, it's important to be able to operate in the weeds as well as at 10,000 feet. What I mean by that is, the plan should include all the nitty-gritty detail as well as the bigger-picture actions. It should also be designed so that it's just as easy to see the little bits of admin you need to do as it is to see how those bits of admin are feeding into your vision: your perfect working life.

If you can't get into the weeds – the detail – when required, that's an indication the action plan hasn't been thought through properly. You may stumble. If you can't rise up to 10,000 feet, you may miss something that you can only see from up there. Creating a successful action plan where you can do both is a difficult skill, but the more you work on it, the better you'll become at it.

SMART Actions

You may have come across the acronym SMART, originally coined by management consultant George T. Doran and now commonly used in the business world. It's essentially a checklist of principles that you want your actions to heed. Different people use slightly different terms for some of the letters in the acronym, but in the version we'll use, SMART stands for:

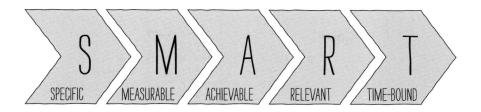

If every single one of your actions is SMART, your action plan will be hyper-effective, and you'll be more likely to complete the action – a win all round.

Let's look at those terms in more detail. As we do, we'll build up a completely SMART action.

Each action in your plan should be **Specific**. There can be no doubt as to what you mean or what you have to do.

Let's say you've decided you need to brush up on your statistics and do a course. Let's start with defining the course you're going to do.

An example of a SPECIFIC action would be: Study the Pearson Business Statistics Level 3 course.

Straight away this is specific – you're clear on which course you're going to study.

Each action should be **Measurable**. A measurable goal has an outcome that can be assessed, either on a sliding scale (1–10) or as a hit or miss, success or failure. It should address questions such as:

- How much?
- How many?
- How will I know when it is accomplished?

An example of a SPECIFIC and MEASURABLE action would be: *Pass* the Pearson Business Statistics Level 3 course.

This is now measurable. You'll know whether or not you've passed, so you'll know when you've delivered your action.

Each action should be **Achievable**. There's no point creating tasks you know you can't deliver. That's just going to demotivate you and waste your time. Pick actions which will stretch you, but which you believe you can achieve.

An example of a SPECIFIC, MEASURABLE and ACHIEVABLE action would be: Pass the Pearson Business Statistics Level 3 course and *achieve over 70 per cent in the final exam.*

Getting 70 per cent is just about you. If you study hard enough, then you can achieve the grade. Compare this with aiming to come top of the class. That depends on who else is in your study group. It might not be achievable.

Your actions should be directly **Relevant** to delivering your goals.

1. Every goal should have at least one action against it.
3. Every action should support the delivery of at least one of your goals.

An example of a SPECIFIC, MEASURABLE, ACHIEVABLE and RELEVANT action would be: Complete the Pearson Business Statistics Level 3 course and achieve over 70 per cent in the final exam, *to support my next promotion.*

Connecting your actions to specific goals helps you to stay focused and on track.

Time-bound means that the action has a deadline. It's so easy to tell yourself that you'll get around to it, find some time next week, or next month. We've all done that and then never found the time! You need a deadline to give you focus and to hold your feet to the fire.

An example of a SPECIFIC, MEASURABLE, ACHIEVABLE, RELEVANT and TIME-BOUND action would be: Complete the Pearson Business Statistics Level 3 course and achieve over 70 per cent in the final exam, *by the end of the calendar year*, to support my promotion *next spring*.

Now you know what you're going to do, how you'll know you've done it, why you're going to do it and when you're going to do it by. This is a powerful action that will help you make significant forward progress.

Exercise 1: Creating Your Actions

Let's start creating some actions to go against each of your goals. Try to reflect the SMART principles, but don't worry too much at this stage – we'll come back and check against these as we work through the exercises.

Fill in the goals you wrote before (see page 118) in the following table. Against each of your goals list three to five actions that you can complete to deliver the goal. These should be exhaustive – delivering all the actions should mean you achieve the goal. Sometimes that could mean you have more than five actions, but try to keep to as short and manageable a list as possible. That will help you later when you're focusing on delivering your plan.

	GOAL		ACTION
1		1.1	
		1.2	
		1.3	
		1.4	
		1.5	

	GOAL		ACTION
2		2.1	
		2.2	
		2.3	
		2.4	
		2.5	

	GOAL		ACTION
3		3.1	
		3.2	
		3.3	
		3.4	
		3.5	

	GOAL		ACTION
4		4.1	
		4.2	
		4.3	
		4.4	
		4.5	

	GOAL		ACTION
5		5.1	
		5.2	
		5.3	
		5.4	
		5.5	

	GOAL		ACTION
6		6.1	
		6.2	
		6.3	
		6.4	
		6.5	

Now look back at the list. Is each action SMART? Does it conform to all of the SMART principles (see page 178)? Sometimes it's not possible to make every action SMART, but try to get most of the principles to fit.

Is each goal reached if you complete your action plan? Read down the actions list and imagine being successful in delivering all of them. Are you going to achieve your goal or is there anything else you need to do?

Exercise 2: Asking for Help

Now let's look at your actions from two other angles.

How hard are they? Thinking this through in advance can help you anticipate the challenges ahead. If all of your actions are hard to do, then you might want to think about revising your approach to make your plan a bit more achievable.

Do you need anyone else to help you complete each action? It's good to have help and support, and you can use this column to focus on where you're going to need it. You may also find that one person can help you with several actions.

To assess your answers to these questions, copy out the actions from the previous exercise in the table below, then fill in the two additional columns.

	ACTION	WILL IT BE EASY, MODERATELY STRAIGHTFORWARD OR HARD TO COMPLETE?	DO YOU NEED ANYONE ELSE TO HELP YOU DO IT? IF SO, WHO?
1.1			
1.2			
1.3			
1.4			
1.5			

	ACTION	WILL IT BE EASY, MODERATELY STRAIGHTFORWARD OR HARD TO COMPLETE?	DO YOU NEED ANYONE ELSE TO HELP YOU DO IT? IF SO, WHO?
2.1			
2.2			
2.3			
2.4			
2.5			

	ACTION	WILL IT BE EASY, MODERATELY STRAIGHTFORWARD OR HARD TO COMPLETE?	DO YOU NEED ANYONE ELSE TO HELP YOU DO IT? IF SO, WHO?
3.1			
3.2			
3.3			
3.4			
3.5			

	ACTION	WILL IT BE EASY, MODERATELY STRAIGHTFORWARD OR HARD TO COMPLETE?	DO YOU NEED ANYONE ELSE TO HELP YOU DO IT? IF SO, WHO?
4.1			
4.2			
4.3			
4.4			
4.5			

	ACTION	WILL IT BE EASY, MODERATELY STRAIGHTFORWARD OR HARD TO COMPLETE?	DO YOU NEED ANYONE ELSE TO HELP YOU DO IT? IF SO, WHO?
5.1			
5.2			
5.3			
5.4			
5.5			

	ACTION	WILL IT BE EASY, MODERATELY STRAIGHTFORWARD OR HARD TO COMPLETE?	DO YOU NEED ANYONE ELSE TO HELP YOU DO IT? IF SO, WHO?
6.1			
6.2			
6.3			
6.4			
6.5			

Exercise 3: Drawing Up Your Timeline

Look again at your actions and assess when you need to complete each one. Which actions do you need to address right now, as soon as you put your pen down? You don't want to drown in an immediate to-do list, so stick with five to ten 'Now!' actions. We want to get on and start making progress, and this will help you create a subset of actions that you can get straight into. Choose ones that will help you accelerate forward.

> # IF YOU HAVE TIME TO MAKE ONLY ONE STEP FORWARD, MAKE IT A BIG ONE.
>
> ## THE IDEA MINDSET

For the other actions, decide whether each needs to happen within three months, within twelve months or by a specific date.

	ACTION	I NEED TO DO THIS			
		NOW! (5-10 ACTIONS)	WITHIN 3 MONTHS	WITHIN 12 MONTHS	BY A SPECIFIC DATE (SPECIFY)
1.1					
1.2					
1.3					
1.4					
1.5					

	ACTION	I NEED TO DO THIS			
		NOW! (5-10 ACTIONS)	WITHIN 3 MONTHS	WITHIN 12 MONTHS	BY A SPECIFIC DATE (SPECIFY)
2.1					
2.2					
2.3					
2.4					
2.5					

	ACTION	I NEED TO DO THIS			
		NOW! (5–10 ACTIONS)	WITHIN 3 MONTHS	WITHIN 12 MONTHS	BY A SPECIFIC DATE (SPECIFY)
3.1					
3.2					
3.3					
3.4					
3.5					

	ACTION	I NEED TO DO THIS			
		NOW! (5-10 ACTIONS)	WITHIN 3 MONTHS	WITHIN 12 MONTHS	BY A SPECIFIC DATE (SPECIFY)
4.1					
4.2					
4.3					
4.4					
4.5					

YOUR ACTION PLAN

	ACTION	NOW! (5–10 ACTIONS)	WITHIN 3 MONTHS	WITHIN 12 MONTHS	BY A SPECIFIC DATE (SPECIFY)
		I NEED TO DO THIS			
5.1					
5.2					
5.3					
5.4					
5.5					

	ACTION	I NEED TO DO THIS			
		NOW! (5–10 ACTIONS)	WITHIN 3 MONTHS	WITHIN 12 MONTHS	BY A SPECIFIC DATE (SPECIFY)
6.1					
6.2					
6.3					
6.4					
6.5					

Now, let's write down your deadlines. We'll use these in your Power Move to Create the Calendar (see page 204).

YOUR DEADLINES:

THE DATE TODAY: ....

....

THE DATE IN THREE MONTHS' TIME: ....

....

THE DATE IN TWELVE MONTHS' TIME: ....

....

You now have an action plan, with SMART objectives, aligned with your vision and goals – a huge achievement.

It might not have been easy, but now that you've developed all four tenets of the IDEA Mindset through the work you've done on your **Identity**, **Direction**, **Engagement** and **Authenticity**, you've got the fundamental roadmap you need to start making real change happen in your working life.

Power Move 1: Create the Calendar

This Power Move is easy. Simply put reminders in your diary, flagging what you need to have done, by when, against the deadline dates from the previous exercise. Then, for every action, put another reminder one to two weeks before the deadline, to prompt you to finish anything off that you haven't quite completed yet.

Great! Now you know what you need to do when you walk out of the room today, and you have reminders in your calendar over the next few months to keep you on track.

Power Move 2: Make an Irreversible Commitment

You know when you're going down a slide at the water park – there's that feeling when you've just launched yourself from the top and there's no going back? You tuck your elbows in and ride the water jet all the way to the bottom.

Too often when we're making change happen we dip one toe in the water and keep the other foot firmly planted on dry land. But at some point you have to let go and jump in with both feet!

This Power Move is about making an irreversible commitment. That's making an action that is impossible to go back on. Use it for something really tough; maybe something you've been putting off for a while, or something that is a daunting hurdle in front of you.

How can you make a commitment truly irreversible? Here are a few ideas for how to incentivise yourself to follow through on your commitment:

- Post your commitment to all your friends on social media.
- Pair up with someone else who is also trying to follow through with a commitment and be each other's 'accountability buddy'.
- Invest an amount of money in the initiative that you're not prepared to lose.
- Commit to an embarrassing (or expensive) forfeit if you fail to follow through with your commitment (a lovely gift to your worst enemy is a very motivating forfeit!).

So, what's your irreversible commitment? This is the action you're committed to taking on – sorting out your taxes; having the difficult conversation with your boss; running the half-marathon.

YOUR COMMITMENT:

....

....

....

....

....

HOW HAVE YOU MADE THIS COMMITMENT IRREVERSIBLE?
WHAT HAVE YOU DONE OR PLEDGED TO DO IF YOU
DON'T FOLLOW THROUGH ON YOUR COMMITMENT?
(YOU CAN'T WRITE SOMETHING HERE IF YOU HAVEN'T
ALREADY MADE YOUR COMMITMENT IRREVERSIBLE.
DON'T GIVE YOURSELF THE OPTION OF BACKING OUT.)

....

....

....

....

....

Week 4: Action Plan – Reflections

Congratulations for reaching the end of Week 4! This is a good moment to take a breath and reflect on what you've done so far.

Having your action plan in place is a big step, but by now you have so much more than just a list of tasks that will lead you to your perfect working life. This is where you should really start to feel your mindset shifting. A new clarity, a new confidence.

Many programmes would stop at this point, the implication being that you can just go ahead and deliver your action plan, and all will be well. But you and I know it's not as easy as that. If it were, crash diets would work, cramming the night before the exam would make you an expert on the subject and getting promoted would be a doddle.

We humans are creatures of habit – we seek comfort in old routines – and while we accomplish seemingly impossible feats, we can lose motivation, confidence and energy, because that's what it is to be human. That's why following through on a plan, even if the end point is our dream career or our longed-for life, is hard. Just because all your actions are in your diary, that doesn't necessarily mean they're going to happen. Unless …

What we're going to do in the next week is ensure that your action plan is something you *can* make happen and make stick. What are the emotional ups and downs you're going to have to navigate when things inevitably don't go perfectly to plan? What are the things you can't plan for that could trip you up? We're going to future-proof your action plan.

> 'It does not do to leave a live dragon out of your calculations, if you live near him.'
>
> J.R.R. TOLKIEN

Your IDEA Mindset: self-reflection

As with the previous weeks, you're going to score yourself on how far you think you've moved forward on each of the IDEA Mindset components compared with where you were at the start of this week. Remember the definitions:

Identity

Clarity about who you are, what you stand for and the issues that are important to you. What your strengths are and the situations in which you excel. How others perceive you and whether that chimes with how you feel about yourself. A sense of self-assurance, an inner compass.

Direction

Clarity about the path ahead of you, what your long-term career goals are and knowing which way you'd turn when faced with a choice. Making forward progress along the path to your perfect career. A sense of comfort with the decisions you've made.

Engagement

Your level of connection with your life and work. How enthusiastic you are about the day ahead and how much of a sense of fulfilment you feel at the end of the day. You are excited about possible career opportunities ahead. Maybe you can see a path to a situation you'd love to be in.

Authenticity

Clarity about how your behaviour and choices at work connect with your values and sense of purpose. Your level of emotional connection with your life and work. Your passion. You're clear on why you're doing what you're doing, or, if not, you're starting to shape a path to an authentic future career.

Put a plus symbol in the appropriate box of the diagram below if you think you've moved forward on one or more of these IDEA Mindset components with the work you've done this week. Put more than one plus if you think you've moved forward a lot. Think about the way you've felt at work, and about the conversations you've had with friends and colleagues. Do you think your mindset is changing?

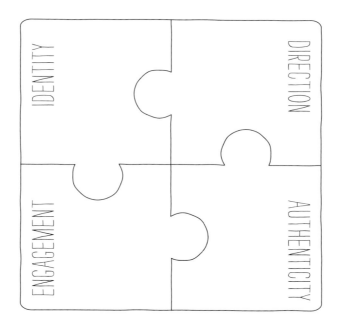

Remember to write some notes in your Reflective Journal (see page 86). Write about how you found this week and if there's anything that you notice is changing in your life and work as you continue on this journey.

Accountability Memo

You're continuing to put new actions in place – new regular habits, new routines, new behaviours. Use this Accountability Memo to capture a list of all the things you're doing today which you weren't doing when you started reading the book. It'll help you to keep hold of those new actions and stay accountable.

....

....

....

....

....

....

....

....

....

....

....

....

....

TAKEAWAY THOUGHT: Writing an action plan is easy. Writing an action plan that delivers all of your goals is harder. Look for any gaps ... and fill them. Keep coming back to your action plan and update it as things change.

WEEK 5

MAKE IT STICK

Well done for making it this far. Just two weeks to go!

You've designed your perfect working life and you know what you need to do to get there. You should already be starting the 'Now!' actions that you wrote into your action plan (see page 197). This week, we're going to get you into a positive headspace that'll set you up for success as you move into realising your career dreams and unlocking your IDEA Mindset. There'll be a moment sometime soon when things will start to click and you'll see all four of the IDEA components coming together. Maybe you're experiencing that a bit already.

So now we're going to look at your plan through a variety of different lenses. We're going to test whether some of your earlier assumptions or decisions still apply and make sense. Don't be afraid to go back and tweak your work if that's the right thing to do. You're building up the layers of a thoughtful and meaningful plan – it's absolutely normal to develop your thinking; in fact, it's a sign that you're truly engaging with the work you're doing here.

There are three exercises you're going to complete this week.

First, we'll look at **Setting Yourself Up for Success** (see page 215). We'll revisit what motivates you and smash the psychological barriers to creating change at work.

Next, we'll move on to **How Will It Feel?** (see page 223): the emotional journey of personal change.

Finally, we're going to plan for **Escaping from the Quicksand** (see page 232). We know that the journey ahead isn't always going to feel easy. When you're in the difficult low points, what can you draw on to get yourself out and onto the next stage?

This week your two Power Moves are:

1. Note Your Emotions (see page 233)
2. Train Your Brain (see page 234)

SOUNDTRACK TO YOUR WEEK

This week's soundtrack is about generating forward drive and momentum.

Play this track before you start the week's reading and exercises to get you in the mood: 'Something's Coming' from *West Side Story*, sung by Mandy Patinkin. The message of this song still resonates over 50 years after it was first written. The syncopations and cross rhythms create that feeling of pushing forward. Find the recording from Mandy Patinkin's *Experiment* album.

Play this track on repeat in the background when you're doing your reading, thinking and writing: '*Nuvole Bianche*' by Ludovico Einaudi, played by Rousseau. Listen to this simple and beautiful piano piece, with its repeated melodic motif, as you think about intentionally turning positive actions into habit.

Play this track when you're done, in celebration of completion and to provide the uplifting energy you need to move on to the next step: 'Paradise' by Coldplay. This hypnotic and uplifting track embodies the sense of drive and momentum we feel as we pursue our dreams. Look for the stadium version recorded live in Paris in 2012.

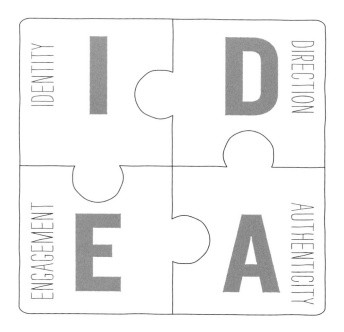

Exercise 1: Setting Yourself Up for Success

Let's start to work through the process of creating change. We'll begin with some of the common reasons why people start with the best intentions and then fail to deliver.

When Mildred and I eventually made it to Italy to advance our ballroom career, we reflected on why we hadn't gone earlier. We'd always wanted to be the best we could be, but when we thought about it we'd allowed ourselves to be hemmed in by constraints of our own making. 'We can't afford to travel abroad regularly.' 'We can't make our jobs flexible enough to make it work.' 'That's something that other, luckier people can do – people with sponsorship.' In reality, nothing about our personal circumstances changed to enable us to go to Italy. We didn't have more money. We didn't have more time. We just decided to make it work. The trigger for the change in our thinking was having been pushed to the limit and knowing that either something needed to change or we had to quit. We had never before had such a stark choice. And it was that stark choice that stopped us from making excuses.

After retiring from dancing, I spent less time worrying about what could go wrong if I decided on a particular course of action and more time thinking about what opportunities could open up. When my boss asked me to run a big project in an area where I didn't have a great deal of experience, I leapt at the opportunity, choosing to view it as a steep learning curve. Before, I would have worried about my relative lack of expertise in managing direct reports or a big budget. Despite accepting the challenge with a positive mindset, it still felt at the time like I was stepping into the unknown and I experienced serious imposter syndrome. But when I looked back, doing something that took me well outside of my comfort zone helped me to lead better and accelerated my career to the next level.

Successful and enduring change doesn't happen by accident. It requires a number of elements to work together in harmony. When change fails, as it often does, you can usually look back and identify the one or two specific elements that caused it to fail.

Let's look at some common excuses for 'why it didn't work':

- 'This all feels like a lot of hard work for not a whole lot of reward.'
- 'I'm not clear on what to do next.'
- 'I don't have time for all this additional work.'

- 'I've been at this for ages and I'm tired – I can't see a light at the end of the tunnel.'
- 'It was good at the beginning, but the longer it went on, the more complicated it got and now I just feel overwhelmed.'
- 'Something else became a bigger priority and then I lost focus.'
- 'I'm fearful of losing the good things I have today.'
- 'I lost confidence in my ability to be good at the job once I got it … so I stopped trying to reach for it.'
- 'I don't think I deserve success.'

As you can see, making change can be pretty daunting! The good news is, you've already done so much by getting this far.

Let's revisit your sense of purpose and get you feeling revved up for the road ahead.

1: Lead with your vision and purpose

No one's going to make your perfect work set-up happen except you. You've got to *know* that this life overhaul is going to be worth it. What's your big reason to want to change – to *need* to change – your work and your life? If you can't find this urgency, then you will drift back into your old ways sooner than you expect.

Let's revisit your career vision and purpose (see page 105) and think about how both will galvanise you. Consider again: why make this change to your working life? Why now? Why aren't you going back to the way things were?

YOUR VISION ... AND WHY IT MOTIVATES YOU TO CHANGE:

....

....

....

YOUR PURPOSE ... AND WHY IT MOTIVATES YOU TO CHANGE:

....

....

....

2: Form your team

You need a close team around you for guidance, moral support and encouragement as you go on this journey. Your first port of call might be the colleagues, friends and family that you've already shared your journey with as part of the programme. Think about anyone else you haven't yet talked to that you might want to bring into your circle at the right time – friends on social media, mentors, old bosses, ex-colleagues, online networks for people in the same line of work as you.

Hold these people close; keep them engaged and involved. They'll help you, they'll motivate you, they'll keep you going through the most difficult times.

> ## WHO ARE THE PEOPLE IN YOUR CLOSE TEAM?
>
> ....
>
> ....
>
> ....

Now think about your extended team. Who are the people that you will draw on from time to time for advice, support and expertise to make individual components of your plan happen? These might be people you've not been in touch with before, such as a subject-matter expert or someone you can partner with to get one of your actions done.

> ## WHO ARE THE PEOPLE IN YOUR EXTENDED TEAM?
>
> ....
>
> ....
>
> ....

3: Remove the barriers

Where are the trip hazards? Where are your blind spots? Anticipating troubles ahead and taking pre-emptive action is a brilliant strategy to help you achieve your career goals.

This step is important. It's for those times when you get stuck, even though all your plans have been drawn up. This might be because 'life takes over'; you might be busy; unexpected stuff might happen which grabs your attention and focus. It might be because you're anxious about a part of the plan and you keep putting it off. It might be because you don't have the full support of everyone in your close team and you're avoiding that difficult conversation.

Let's think about what those barriers to change might be:

- Not enough time
- Not enough money
- Distraction
- Lack of energy
- Personal (internal) conflict
- Conflict with others
- Lack of confidence
- Fear
- Inertia
- Past failure

Sound familiar?

Revisit your action plan (see page 197) and then highlight what barriers you think might be ahead of you and how you might overcome them. It might help to think about the kinds of barriers that have held you up in the past. Not every hurdle can be removed from the road ahead, but each one that you can eliminate makes your journey easier.

This is a real honesty moment – you know yourself better than anyone else, and the most important things to work through here are also going to be the most difficult things to face. Be true to yourself and you'll give yourself the best chance of success.

WHAT ARE THE BIGGEST BARRIERS TO CHANGE IN YOUR WORKING LIFE? WHAT'S HELD YOU BACK IN THE PAST?

....

....

....

WHAT WILL YOU DO TO OVERCOME THOSE HURDLES?

....

....

....

4: Generate quick wins

Getting a few quick wins under our belt helps get us off to a flying start and keeps us motivated when the going gets tough. That's why we're doing the Power Moves at the end of each week.

You should have started your 'Now!' actions in your action plan already (see page 197). If you're beginning to see the positive impact of making those early changes, reflect back on what you've noticed has changed as a result.

WHAT HAVE YOU STARTED DOING FOR THE FIRST
TIME AND WHAT IMPACT HAVE YOU SEEN?

....

....

....

5: Create new habits

You're sitting in pole position on the racetrack. The lights go out and you thump your foot down on the accelerator pedal. It's no good getting from 0 to 60 in under three seconds if the engine cuts out and you drift to a stop before the first corner. Sustaining acceleration is critical to change, otherwise all those quick wins were for nothing.

You thought about creating some new habits at the end of Week 1 (see page 89). Check back now to what you wrote then. How's it going? Do you need to work on making those habits stick? If not, what have you noticed to be different since you started that activity?

ONE EXAMPLE OF A NEW HABIT YOU'VE CREATED
AND WHAT IMPACT IT'S HAVING:

....

....

....

....

....

Exercise 2: How Will It Feel?

Now we're going to look at the emotional journey of change.

There will be ups and downs – in the short term, quite possibly more downs than ups! It's easy to feel alone when you're in the dips, as though your journey to your perfect working life is uniquely difficult. In fact, we all experience very similar feelings when we're navigating big changes in our lives. These feelings are best illustrated by what's known as the change curve.

The change curve

There have been a few attempts over the years to articulate the emotional journey of change, beginning with the work of psychiatrist and author Elisabeth Kübler-Ross on grief in 1969.[11] Psychologist John Fisher built on Kübler-Ross's research in 1999 in the context of how individuals responded to changes at work. The following figure is a simplified version of what he called the Personal Transition Curve, now commonly referred to as the change curve, which illustrates the various stages of transition we go through when we experience change.[12]

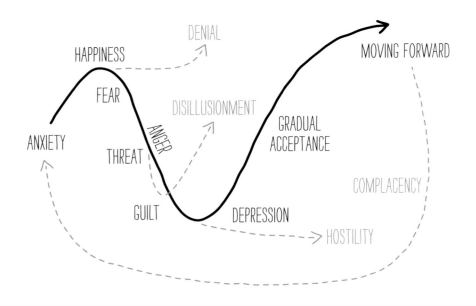

On seeing this diagram, one of my friends said to me, 'It's like you've been inside my head for the last three years!' These emotional ups and downs can feel very lonely, until you realise that lots of people around you are on a similar path.

Let's walk through the different stages as shown in the change curve.

The initial step, **Anxiety**, reflects that sense of uncertainty at the start of the journey. It's that moment when you know something's not right in your current working life, that something needs to change. You're not yet clear on what that is and what the process of change might look like, nor where you might end up. This can be an anxious and unsettling time.

'Something's got to change. I don't know where I'm heading, but wherever it is, it's got to be better than where I am today.'

SOMETIMES YOU DON'T
SEE HOW DEEP THE
VALLEY WAS UNTIL
YOU'RE AT THE TOP OF
THE MOUNTAIN.

THE IDEA MINDSET

As you start to process that something about your current work set-up needs to change and that you need to take steps to face it, you reach an initial stage of **Happiness**. You're finally doing something about the problem and you're actively taking back control.

*'I've accepted something needs to change and I've bought
a book to help me do something about it. I'm on the up!'*

This is the first point at which you can shoot off the curve into a dead
end. **Denial**.

*'Turns out, all I needed to do was to buy that book and face my situation.
Maybe my job isn't so bad after all. I'm sure things will get better.'*

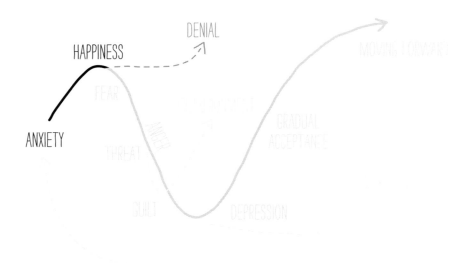

Stop at this point and you'll likely be back where you started in no time.
If you push through and make progress with your action plan, then that
improved working environment on the horizon will start to feel a bit
more real. But now you might start to experience a sense of **Fear** about
the journey ahead.

*'This is a bit out of my comfort zone. What if I've read the situation wrong?
What if I end up in a worse situation than the one I started in?'*

You're getting onto the downward slope now and at this stage you might start to experience a sense of **Anger** or **Threat**. Initially these emotions can be directed more at others than yourself.

> *'I shouldn't be in this situation at work where I feel like*
> *I have to change jobs. It's my manager's fault for not*
> *doing their job properly and looking out for me.'*

This is the second point at which you can shoot off the curve into a dead end. **Disillusionment**. In struggling with the challenges ahead, you return to where you started.

> *'This is too much risk. I can't deal with going*
> *through all this change. I'm stuck with a bad situation*
> *and I'm just going to have to put up with it.'*

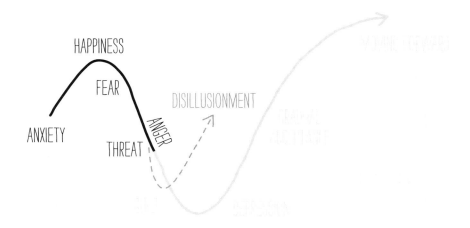

Stop at this point and you'll find it much harder to get going again. If you push on with your action plan, it might still feel worse before it feels better. That sense of **Anger** or **Threat** can transition further into **Guilt**.

'Maybe it's partly my fault that I'm in this situation with work. I'd have been in a better place if I had pursued a different career path from the beginning.'

Ultimately the combination of emotions can spiral into **Depression** and the dead end of **Hostility**.

'I'm going to go back and have a face-to-face with my boss, tell him what I think about the situation he's landed me in. I shouldn't have to change just because he's ruined my prospects.'

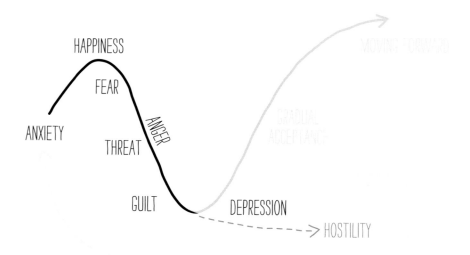

Stop at this point and it's really hard to get back on track. Feelings of hostility, bitterness and resentment can be difficult to turn into positive, self-directed motivation for the future.

This is the moment when you must decide that you're taking control and creating the future you want. It's up from here on. Make it through this step and you will begin to move through **Gradual Acceptance** into **Moving Forward**.

'This is really happening. I'm glad I put this career change in motion. The future is going to be brighter and better than I could have hoped for. I feel positive and energised – I did this.'

But you still have to take care. This is the fourth point at which you can shoot off the curve and fire yourself back to the beginning. **Complacency**.

'I've done it. Work is going to be great now. All I've got to do is keep sticking to my new routine. Which is hard with the kids. And my partner is going through some stuff at their work. And … oh I just slipped back into that old habit. And that one. Oh …'

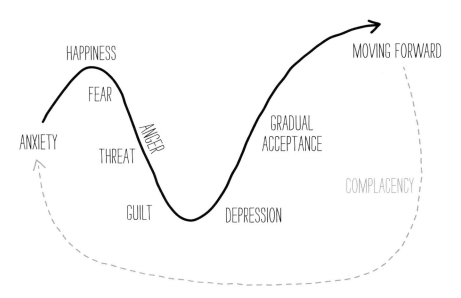

This is perhaps the hardest bit of all. Making change happen is hard. Making it stick is much harder. You have to change your life, your focus, your routine. You need the support of those around you. You need to be able to navigate the inevitable bumps in the road towards your new working life. If you stop trying at this stage, you can easily find yourself back where you started. Not necessarily in the exact same situation – maybe you've changed your role or you've moved to a new company. But the issues and frustrations that you were experiencing at the start will show themselves in your new situation if you haven't managed to address the fundamental root causes.

That's why a vision, goals and an action plan are not in themselves enough to guarantee you success. You need a holistic approach, setting yourself up for success in every way – physically, mentally, emotionally, behaviourally. That holistic approach is at the heart of the IDEA Mindset. You know you're never going back to how it used to be.

Use the Accountability Memo at the end of each week to stay on track with those new actions, habits, routines and behaviours that you weren't doing before you started reading this book.

WHERE ARE YOU ON THE CHANGE CURVE NOW AND WHAT DOES IT FEEL LIKE?

....

....

....

....

....

WHAT COMES NEXT ON THE CHANGE CURVE?
HOW WILL YOU NAVIGATE IT?

....

....

....

....

....

WHAT STUCK OUT TO YOU AS YOU READ ABOUT
THE EMOTIONAL JOURNEY OF CHANGE?

....

....

....

....

....

Exercise 3: Escaping from the Quicksand

Do you remember quicksand in the old films? The hero or heroine would be running from danger and suddenly find themselves in the middle of a swamp, slowly sinking. If they stood completely still, then they stopped sinking, but as soon as they moved they slipped further down. Most of the time, help was coming and they found a way to carefully extract themselves. Rule number one with quicksand: don't panic, don't struggle!

On your journey towards change, the dips in the change curve can feel like quicksand. Guilt, depression, hostility – they can suck you down, and when you struggle you get pulled further in. When you're in those dips, what techniques can you apply to help ease yourself out of the danger and onto dry land?

Could you take a break and come back to the problem with a fresh perspective?

Could you connect with a friend and get an alternative point of view to challenge your thinking?

Could you reflect on the positive affirmation you wrote at the end of Week 3 (see page 167)?

Does writing down your thoughts help to rationalise how you're feeling and help you put it in perspective?

WHAT IS YOUR TOP STRATEGY FOR GETTING OUT OF THE QUICKSAND?

....

....

....

....

....

Power Move I: Note Your Emotions

We've talked a bit already about removing the barriers (see page 220). In this Power Move you're going to work on becoming more aware of your emotions. Building self-awareness will help you manage your emotions as you navigate the change curve and find that calm clarity of the IDEA Mindset. Use your Reflective Journal to help you do this (see page 86).

When a situation arises at work which stimulates an emotional response, try to hold the thoughts that crop up in your head. Whenever you have an opportunity, make some notes in your Reflective Journal.

- What was the situation? Where were you? Who was there? What was said?

- What was it specifically that triggered your emotional response? What happened immediately before you noticed it?
- What emotions did you feel? How intense were they? Try to write as much as possible on this.
- How long did the heightened emotion last?
- What did it take to get you back on track?
- Is this something you've experienced before? In what circumstances does it tend to show up?

Once you've done that a few times, step back and look for the patterns. The main goal in this exercise is simply to become more aware of your own emotions, but it's helpful if you can also start to understand what triggers you as well.

'Our feelings are our most genuine paths to knowledge. They are chaotic, sometimes painful, sometimes contradictory, but they come from deep within us.'

AUDRE LORDE, WRITER AND ACTIVIST

Power Move 2: Train Your Brain

Ever find that your brain is tricking you into thinking a situation is worse than it really is? We're experts at creating these 'Thinking Traps'. With a bit of practice, you can turn that negative spiral into a positive.

Thinking Traps are well recognised in psychology.[13] In this Power Move, we're going to look at some of the most common and explore how you might turn each into a positive.

Thinking Trap 1: Mind-reading

Mind-reading is when you *assume* you know what someone else is thinking, and either get down on yourself or make poor decisions off the back of it.

What it sounds like:

> *'They've already decided I'm not going to get the job.'*

What it *could* sound like:

> *'This is my chance to convince them I'm the best candidate. Maybe I'll surprise them.'*

DO YOU RECOGNISE MIND-READING IN YOURSELF?

WHAT DOES THIS NEGATIVE INNER CHATTER
SOUND LIKE IN YOUR LIFE?

....

....

....

HOW COULD YOU TURN IT INTO A POSITIVE?

....

....

....

Thinking Trap 2: Filtering

Filtering is when you filter out all the good stuff because someone said something negative. It's a quick way to lose motivation.

What it sounds like:

> *'That critical comment proves that no one enjoyed my presentation.'*

What it *could* sound like:

> *'I know that one person didn't like my presentation, but I don't know what the others in the room thought.'*

DO YOU RECOGNISE FILTERING IN YOURSELF?

WHAT DOES THIS NEGATIVE INNER CHATTER
SOUND LIKE IN YOUR LIFE?

....

....

....

HOW COULD YOU TURN IT INTO A POSITIVE?

....

....

....

Thinking Trap 3: Labelling

Labelling is when you decide that one incident defines you:
    What it sounds like:

> *'I failed that time. I'm a failure.'*

What it *could* sound like:

> *'I failed that time, but I learned something for next time.'*

DO YOU RECOGNISE LABELLING IN YOURSELF?

....

WHAT DOES THIS NEGATIVE INNER CHATTER
SOUND LIKE IN YOUR LIFE?

....

....

....

HOW COULD YOU TURN IT INTO A POSITIVE?

....

....

....

Thinking Trap 4: Emotional reasoning

Emotional reasoning is where you make decisions based on how you feel, not on what the evidence tells you is true.

What it sounds like:

> *'I'm not sure I'm up to this. I won't do it.'*

What it *could* sound like:

> *'What can I do to build up my confidence before I tackle this?'*

DO YOU RECOGNISE EMOTIONAL REASONING IN YOURSELF?

....

WHAT DOES THIS NEGATIVE INNER CHATTER
SOUND LIKE IN YOUR LIFE?

....

....

....

HOW COULD YOU TURN IT INTO A POSITIVE?

....

....

....

Thinking Trap 5: Fallacy of fairness

The fallacy of fairness is when you're resentful of what happens to others because you believe life should be fair … even when it sometimes just isn't.
What it sounds like:

'My friend got a great job offer with more pay. I should have more pay.'

What it *could* sound like:

'My friend got a great job offer. I'm happy for her. It's inspired me to go look for my next opportunity.'

DO YOU RECOGNISE THE FALLACY OF FAIRNESS IN YOURSELF?

....

WHAT DOES THIS NEGATIVE INNER CHATTER
SOUND LIKE IN YOUR LIFE?

....

....

....

HOW COULD YOU TURN IT INTO A POSITIVE?

....

....

....

Week 5: Make It Stick – Reflections

Humans are by nature fallible, emotional, irrational. We're not robots, and we don't make change happen like robots. Input A, Output B. We find things hard. We go through peaks and troughs of motivation. Often, we get frustrated at ourselves for not following through on something we meant to do. But that's human nature – no one's perfect, and life would be much duller if there weren't room for failure or for changes in mood or direction.

This week, as all four tenets of the IDEA Mindset continue to develop in parallel and feed into each other, we've worked on recognising, even embracing, our fallibility and figuring out how to stay human while getting things done which take us towards our perfect working life.

Your IDEA Mindset: self-reflection

As with previous weeks, you're going to score yourself on how far you think you've moved forward on each of the IDEA Mindset components compared with where you were at the start of this week. Remember the definitions:

Identity

Clarity about who you are, what you stand for and the issues that are important to you. What your strengths are and the situations in which you excel. How others perceive you and whether that chimes with how you feel about yourself. A sense of self-assurance, an inner compass.

Direction

Clarity about the path ahead of you, what your long-term career goals are and knowing which way you'd turn when faced with a choice. Making forward progress along the path to your perfect career. A sense of comfort with the decisions you've made.

Engagement

Your level of connection with your life and work. How enthusiastic you are about the day ahead and how much of a sense of fulfilment you feel at the end of the day. You are excited about possible career opportunities ahead. Maybe you can see a path to a situation you'd love to be in.

Authenticity

Clarity about how your behaviour and choices at work connect with your values and sense of purpose. Your level of emotional connection with your life and work. Your passion. You're clear on why you're doing what you're doing, or, if not, you're starting to shape a path to an authentic future career.

Put a plus symbol in the appropriate box of the diagram below if you think you've moved forward on one or more of these IDEA Mindset components with the work you've done this week. Put more than one plus if you think you've moved forward a lot. Think about the way you've felt at work, and about the conversations you've had with friends and colleagues. Do you think your mindset is changing?

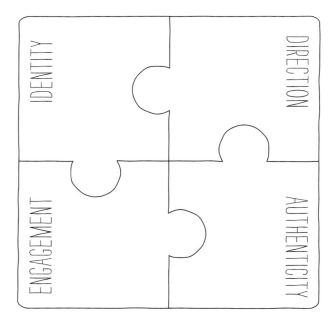

Remember to write some notes in your Reflective Journal (see page 86). Write about how you found this week and if there's anything that you notice is changing in your life and work as you continue on this journey.

Accountability Memo

You're starting to put new actions in place – new regular habits, new routines, new behaviours. Use this Accountability Memo to capture a list of all the things you're doing today which you weren't doing when you started reading the book. It'll help you to keep hold of those new actions and stay accountable.

....

....

....

....

....

....

....

....

....

....

....

....

....

....

....

....

....

....

....

....

....

TAKEAWAY THOUGHT: Don't expect your career-change plans to go right all the time. Your journey will have ups and downs. You can use the change tools we've discovered this week to cope with the difficult times and keep up your forward momentum.

WEEK 6

TELL YOUR STORY

Than is it. You're clear on your vision, purpose and goals, you have your action plan in the calendar, you've got some mental resilience tools and you've thought through how you're going to make it stick. You've already got started with those 'Now!' action points. Maybe you're already starting to see early signs of progress! What's left?

Before we talk about the exercises for this week, let's spend a little time talking about ownership, as it's a concept that taps into every component of the IDEA Mindset: knowing who you are (**Identity**), taking charge of your **Direction**, making choices based on the things you love (**Engagement**) and the things that really matter to you (**Authenticity**) – that's all ownership.

Ownership

I've said it before and I'll say it again: this is *your* plan and only *you* can make it happen. Taking ownership is probably one of the hardest parts of any plan. It's easy to get down on yourself, lose motivation, blame external factors or other people for why you weren't able to make that change to your working life or career happen. But only *you* will change your life.

Maybe you've tried and failed in the past. Maybe you've come up against an insurmountable obstacle. Maybe you've just struggled to have the time, the momentum, the motivation to change careers, departments or how you work.

This time it's going to be different.

This is your time. Even when it's hard, even when the mood doesn't take you, you're going to do it. *You're* going to do it.

Imagine how it's going to feel, that day when it's the norm for you to wake up excited about the day ahead. When you're able to devote as much time as you want and need to each area of your life – no compromises. When you're doing good work that you're proud of every day, with people who inspire you and respect your expertise. When you feel that sense of freedom which comes with knowing exactly how smart and capable you are, knowing that whatever you want to do, now or in the future, you can accomplish it. How are you going to feel in a year's time when you look back and realise how far you've come? Sometimes it can help to cast your mind forward and imagine what the future's going to feel like.

A conversation with yourself

To help you reflect on and connect with that sense of ownership, find a day when you're well rested and don't have other things on your mind. Go on a walk for at least an hour. Maybe early in the morning when the sun is coming up and there aren't many people around. Maybe in that golden hour in the evening when the colours of nature are so beautiful.

Go somewhere that makes you feel very comfortable, maybe somewhere you go to relax or a place that holds happy memories. Sit for a while. Spend that walk thinking about your journey to come and the commitments you've made to yourself and others.

Come back from that walk a new person, with a fresh view on how things are going to change and a feeling of excitement for what awaits you round the corner. You're going to make your future happen and reach your fullest potential.

There are three exercises you're going to complete this week.

First, we'll look at **Talking Points** (see page 255). These are the most significant and memorable changes you're making as you move into your future career plan. You might want these talking points to convey that you're unique, impressive and interesting. Whether you're meeting someone for the first time who you want to impress, particularly in a work context, or if you're simply talking to your boss or colleagues, these are the points you want to get across for them to appreciate your change.

Next, we'll move on to **Building the Narrative** (see page 260). We'll take those talking points and build them into a story that you can adapt and use in different situations to communicate what you want to say about yourself and transform how people who already know you perceive you.

Finally, we're going to **Test Your Story** (see page 265). You don't know if you've got it right until you've gone out there and started talking to people and observed their reaction.

This week your two Power Moves are:

1. Update Your Online Profiles (see page 266)
2. Network and Connect (see page 267)

♫♪ SOUNDTRACK TO YOUR WEEK ♫♪

This week's soundtrack is all about taking ownership and telling your story.

Play this track before you start the week's reading and exercises to get you in the mood: 'Read All About It (Pt III)' by Emeli Sandé. This track inspires us to sing, to shout out our story. Listen to one of the live performances where you get the full, unadulterated emotional release of this powerful song.

Play this track on repeat in the background when you're doing your reading, thinking and writing: 'Now We Are Free' by Hans Zimmer. You may recognise this theme from the film *Gladiator*. The hypnotic soundscape will make you think of a future where your clarity of mind has set you free.

Play this track when you're done, in celebration of completion and to provide the uplifting energy you'll use to maintain momentum for the future: 'One Day Like This' by Elbow. The ultimate song of celebration. As the chorus builds, close your eyes, hold your arms out wide and take in everything you've achieved!

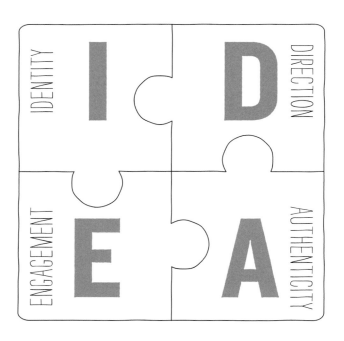

Exercise 1: Talking Points

There are two reasons to tell your story:

1. Telling *yourself* helps you to stay clear and focused on why you're making this change in your working life.
2. Telling *others* helps you stick to your commitments and can amplify the impact of the changes you're making.

> 'You can't control the story if you don't tell your story. As long as this is true, others will define who you are.'
>
> LARRY WRIGHT,
> STAFF WRITER AT
> THE *NEW YORKER*

The people around you are human. They're living their own lives. As a result, it may take them some time to notice in you changes that you might think are obvious. Like a plant growing – from day to day, it looks like the same plant, and then suddenly you'll notice that it seems to be a bit taller than when you first had it. Maybe a bit leafier? You'd only notice the change immediately if it did something striking, like burst into flower.

If you don't bring it to their attention, how long might it take for your colleagues, peers, even close friends and family to notice how much you've built your confidence, how you're managing your time differently, how you're being more productive, how you've become less anxious? (All are by-products of the IDEA Mindset.) Possibly months, not weeks. Maybe not at all. Telling your story is a bit like bursting into flower. You're drawing their attention to something that's different. You're inviting them to see you in a new and different way.

Bringing it to their attention doesn't mean shouting it from the rooftops. There are many ways, some subtle and some less so, that you can help people become aware of how you're changing. You might have a dedicated meeting with them or you might drop it into conversation when you're talking about something else. Alternatively, you might demonstrate how you've changed through what you do, not what you say. Allow them to notice that your manner, your confidence and your choices are different. Perhaps you open a conversation about flexible working, organise your day differently to clear your emails by mid-morning or start to speak up more in the team meeting about your achievements and those of your team.

Of course, you can deliver on your career goals without engaging others in what you're doing and how you're changing. For your plan, it might not be important that others notice and acknowledge your change or consider you differently as a result of it. Often, however, the ultimate outcome of your change – perhaps a promotion, perhaps greater influence, perhaps a better working relationship with those around you – requires others to recognise how you've changed, so they can create, or assist in creating, opportunities for you. These exercises will help you to think through how you might communicate your story to others.

As dancers, Mildred and I were conscious of how long it took to change others' perception of us. Typically, we needed to be performing at a markedly higher level for about six months before a competition judge would come up to us and compliment us on our improvement. This was because, when they glanced across the floor and saw us dancing, their natural reaction was one of recognition, not evaluation. They'd seen us perform dozens of times before. They knew how good we were, so they didn't assess us from scratch each time. For us to change their perception, we had to trigger them to think differently, to see us in a new light. We would use a change in our choreography, a change in our dance style or a change in our look to shock them into changing their perceptions. It was our way of telling a new and different story.

Years later, when I left my corporate career to become a full-time coach, it took six to nine months for many of my former colleagues to recognise that this was a real and permanent career change, and not just another side hustle. Early on, people mainly wanted to talk to me about the jobs I used to have. I needed to change how they perceived me. I changed my job title on LinkedIn, Twitter and Instagram and started posting about coaching topics instead of the latest news in the corporate world. I updated my email footer with my coaching qualifications and studiously avoided getting into conversations that implied I still had one foot in the boardroom. The clearer I was that coaching was my singular focus, the easier it was for former colleagues to change how they thought of me. In time, the people in my corporate network became powerful advocates for me as a coach and I started new coaching partnerships with a number of them.

MAKE THEM LOOK.
MAKE THEM SEE.

THE IDEA MINDSET

What's the message?

Let's start with some exercises that will explore what story you want to be telling and the impact you want it to have. Imagine you're in the head of the person listening to your story. How do you want them to feel about you? What change to your working life do you want them to notice? How do you want their perception of you, or behaviour towards you, to change in light of what you're going to tell them?

WHAT NOTICEABLE DIFFERENCES WILL PEOPLE BE ABLE TO SEE IN YOU WHEN YOU'VE COMPLETED YOUR ACTION PLAN?

HOW WILL YOU FEEL ONCE YOU'VE CHANGED, AND HOW IS THAT DIFFERENT TO HOW YOU FEEL TODAY?

DO YOU WANT SPECIFIC PEOPLE TO SEE YOU
DIFFERENTLY AS YOU CHANGE? WHY?

....

....

....

HOW WOULD YOU SUM UP THE NEXT 12 MONTHS
OF CHANGE TO COME IN ONE SENTENCE?

....

....

....

Exercise 2: Building the Narrative

Now let's start to turn those thoughts into some little storytelling nuggets. Each of these is designed to help you explore how you might tell your story differently in different situations. These become like your box of paints. When you're telling your story, you can reach into your box of paints and pull out the right colour and the right quantity to paint the perfect picture for that moment.

Over time you will refine these nuggets. The best way to work out how to tell your story is ... to tell your story! Over time you'll find language that works and language that doesn't, words that feel true and authentic and others that you find don't convey the impact you want. That's normal – here, you're writing a first draft and you can come back and edit and update it as much as you like.

IF YOU HAD FIVE MINUTES WITH A TRUSTED MENTOR TO TALK ABOUT YOUR UPCOMING CAREER JOURNEY, WHAT WOULD YOU SAY? (WRITE DOWN FOUR TO FIVE SENTENCES):

This narrative prepares you for a one-on-one conversation about your story and the change you're making.

....

....

....

....

....

....

....

....

WHAT WOULD THE 'ABOUT ME' SECTION AT THE TOP OF YOUR CV SAY, NOW YOU'RE IN THE PROCESS OF THIS RADICAL CHANGE? (WRITE DOWN TWO TO THREE SENTENCES):

This narrative is the foundation for a written description of your story and the change you're making. It can be used for people who are considering you for a job.

....

....

....

....

....

....

....

....

....

WHAT WOULD THE BIOGRAPHY PARAGRAPH ON YOUR WEBSITE SAY? (WRITE DOWN FOUR TO FIVE SENTENCES):

This narrative is the foundation for a written description of your story and the change you're making, aimed at people who don't know you personally but are interested to find out more about you.

....

....

....

....

....

....

....

....

....

IF SOMEONE INTRODUCED YOU TO SPEAK AT AN EVENT TODAY, WHAT WOULD YOU LIKE THEM TO SAY? (WRITE DOWN FOUR TO FIVE SENTENCES):

This narrative is the foundation for a short, verbal introduction that highlights why you're unique and worth listening to.

....

....

....

....

....

....

....

....

....

Exercise 3: Testing Your Story

Chat with some of the people who know you best about the journey you're on to your perfect working life. Talk about your career vision and your commitments. Engage with people in person, on the phone, on social media and by email or in writing. Does communicating your story in different ways help you think about how you can make it more compelling and effective?

Capture their thoughts here – how they think the changes to your working life are going to impact you, what changes they're expecting to see, what they're excited about. Does their feedback change your thinking around your story's core messages?

WHAT DID THEY SAY?

....

....

....

....

....

....

```
........................................................

........................................................

........................................................

........................................................

........................................................
```

A big part of your IDEA Mindset is clarity and confidence. With the work you've done here, you should feel well prepared to go out into the world and start talking to people about the journey you're on.

Power Move 1: Update Your Online Profiles

It's a daunting but powerful move, starting to make public your commitment to a new future. A great way of doing that is to update your online profiles. Think about the profile photo you use, your job headline and summary paragraph – the things you highlight in your work experience.

Pressing the button to publish your new profile details is a significant moment.

Press the button!

Power Move 2: Network and Connect

It's a good idea to build your network and make new connections as you move towards your future career. Networking is about making the first contact, but making real connections is about building deep relationships that are meaningful and bring both of you value over time.

Set a commitment to make at least one new connection a week. That'll mean you'll build 50 new connections over the next year, which in turn will create plentiful opportunities and new ways of thinking.

Maybe within your organisation there's a person you've admired from afar but have never really managed a conversation with. Maybe a friend or colleague has suggested someone you ought to meet. If no one comes to mind, talk to people who know you well and ask them if they have ideas around connections you might consider making.

When you first meet a new person, use your talking points (see page 255) and narrative (see page 260 d) to describe who you are and where you're going. Networking conversations should be two-way – remember to ask about them as much as you talk about yourself, and listen to their answers.

Week 6: Ownership and Storytelling – Reflections

We've reached the end of the programme, but not the end of your journey. You'll still have most of your action plan to carry out, and even once you're in your perfect work set-up, what you want will change as you and your circumstances change. Your IDEA Mindset is clear and confident, but it's also flexible and adaptable. You navigate the bumps in the road more easily than before.

This isn't the kind of journey that ends. There's no buffer at the end of the train track where you're going to come to a juddering halt. This is a continuing journey of personal development. As you progress, it will make more and more sense to you. Trust in the process.

You've developed tools and approaches throughout this book which will help you navigate the rest of your life and career. You've learned things about yourself that will stand you in good stead for the future. You'll achieve your goals and set many new ones. You'll evolve your story as you grow and develop.

Your IDEA Mindset: self-reflection

As with the previous weeks, you're going to score yourself on how far you think you've moved forward on each of the IDEA Mindset components compared with where you were at the start of this week. Remember the definitions:

Identity
Clarity about who you are, what you stand for and the issues that are important to you. What your strengths are and the situations in which you excel. How others perceive you and whether that chimes with how you feel about yourself. A sense of self-assurance, an inner compass.

Direction
Clarity about the path ahead of you, what your long-term career goals are and knowing which way you'd turn when faced with a choice. Making forward progress along the path to your perfect career. A sense of comfort with the decisions you've made.

Engagement
Your level of connection with your life and work. How enthusiastic you are about the day ahead and how much of a sense of fulfilment you feel at the end of the day. You are excited about possible career opportunities ahead. Maybe you can see a path to a situation you'd love to be in.

Authenticity

Clarity about how your behaviour and choices at work connect with your values and sense of purpose. Your level of emotional connection with your life and work. Your passion. You're clear on why you're doing what you're doing, or, if not, you're starting to shape a path to an authentic future career.

Put a plus symbol in the appropriate box of the diagram below if you think you've moved forward on one or more of these IDEA Mindset components with the work you've done this week. Put more than one plus if you think you've moved forward a lot. Think about the way you've felt at work, and about the conversations you've had with friends and colleagues. Do you think your mindset is changing?

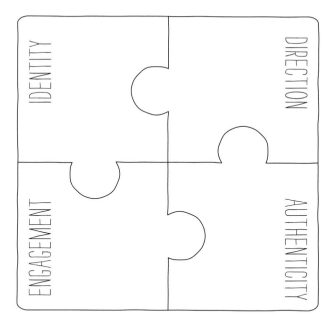

Remember to write some notes in your Reflective Journal (see page 86). Write about how you found this week and if there's anything that you notice is changing in your life and work as you continue on this journey.

Accountability Memo

You're starting to put new actions in place – new regular habits, new routines, new behaviours. Use this Accountability Memo to capture a list of all the things you're doing today which you weren't doing when you started reading the book. It'll help you to keep hold of those new actions and stay accountable.

....

....

....

....

....

....

....

....

TAKEAWAY THOUGHT: The change inside your head is the most important change of all. The impact of that change is amplified if people around you can see it and respond to it. Become an expert at telling your story.

YOUR IDEA PROFILE REVISITED

R emember right back at the start of the programme, you completed your IDEA Profile questionnaire (see page 41)? Your results were used to calculate your 'IDEA Profile' against the four dimensions of **Identity**, **Direction**, **Engagement** and **Authenticity**. Now you're going to complete it again with a transformed perspective.

Don't look back at your old answers!

Your New **IDEA** Profile

For each statement, put a tick in the appropriate column.

IDENTITY	STRONGLY AGREE	AGREE	DISAGREE	STRONGLY DISAGREE
1 I have a clear sense of what makes me unique and of what qualities I share with others				
2 I have a clear sense of my personal values				
3 I have a clear sense of how people senior to me perceive me				
4 I have a clear sense of how my peers/colleagues/ friends perceive me				
5 I have a clear sense of how people junior to me perceive me				
SCORE FOR EACH TICK	+2	+1	-1	-2
TOTAL SCORE				

DIRECTION	STRONGLY AGREE	AGREE	DISAGREE	STRONGLY DISAGREE
1 I am clear on my long-term goals				
2 I am clear on the major steps I need to take to reach them				
3 I am clear on where I am going next				
4 I have developed a simple action plan				
5 I am making good progress with my action plan				
SCORE FOR EACH TICK	+2	+1	−1	−2
TOTAL SCORE				

ENGAGEMENT	STRONGLY AGREE	AGREE	DISAGREE	STRONGLY DISAGREE
1 When I get up in the morning I am usually enthusiastic about the day ahead				
2 When I go to sleep I usually feel a sense of achievement for what I have done in the day				
3 I am doing a job that is right for me				
4 I work with people who bring out the best in me and I actively seek out people like this to work with				
5 I like to tell other people about the work I do				
SCORE FOR EACH TICK	+2	+1	−1	−2
TOTAL SCORE				

AUTHENTICITY	STRONGLY AGREE	AGREE	DISAGREE	STRONGLY DISAGREE
1 I feel a strong sense of purpose with the work I do				
2 My work aligns with my values – what I consider to be important				
3 I am emotionally engaged – I use my heart as well as my head at work				
4 I develop enduring relationships at work. I take time to listen to colleagues, clients and customers and I am sensitive to the needs of others				
5 I am disciplined in the way I work. I manage my emotions well				
SCORE FOR EACH TICK	+2	+1	–1	–2
TOTAL SCORE				

Totals

Now you've completed the questionnaire, fill in the boxes below with the total scores from each section, then calculate your total for each element.

ELEMENT	STRONGLY AGREE	AGREE	DISAGREE	STRONGLY DISAGREE	TOTAL
EXAMPLE	+4	+1	-2	0	+3
IDENTITY					
DIRECTION					
ENGAGEMENT					
AUTHENTICITY					

Interpretation

WHICH OF THE FOUR ELEMENTS DID YOU SCORE HIGHEST FOR?

....

....

WHICH ELEMENTS DID YOU GET A RELATIVELY LOW SCORE FOR?

....

....

DOES THAT FEEL RIGHT FOR WHERE YOU ARE AS YOU
COMPLETE THE IDEA MINDSET PROGRAMME?

....

....

....

ARE THE RESULTS WHAT YOU EXPECTED
OR WAS ANYTHING A SURPRISE?

....

....

....

....

....

Now let's compare your new results with your score at the start of the programme:

ELEMENT	TOTAL WHEN I STARTED THE PROGRAMME	TOTAL WHEN I COMPLETED THE PROGRAMME
IDENTITY		
DIRECTION		
ENGAGEMENT		
AUTHENTICITY		

If you've got your plan right and worked through all the change elements, you should now score higher on every element than you did at the start. If not, look back through the IDEA Profile questions and consider why you didn't score more strongly in those categories. Do you need to adjust your plan to address a gap?

Reflection

Remember right back at the start of this journey, you went and looked at yourself in the mirror (see page 27)? Go and do it again now. Look at yourself. And keep looking for a whole minute. Can you manage two? Look at yourself, listen to what's going on inside your head, watch yourself. Give yourself your undivided time and attention. Face everything there is to see and know. Don't brush anything under the carpet. This is just about you.

WRITE DOWN SIX WORDS THAT CAME INTO YOUR
HEAD WHEN YOU LOOKED IN THE MIRROR

1. ....

2. ....

3. ....

4. ....

5. ....

6. ....

Now go back and look at the words you wrote the first time you did that exercise early in the book and compare them. What does this tell you?

DRAWING TO A CLOSE

I t's difficult to put into words what a significant piece of work you've completed in finalising your action plan and unlocking your IDEA Mindset. Instead, let's talk about some values that you've shown over the past few weeks:

Honesty and Openness

Change happens only when we're honest with ourselves. What you find hardest to acknowledge and admit to yourself may be the biggest barrier to change. You have to put the big stuff, the difficult stuff, on the table. You've done that here.

Ambition and Motivation

Half-hearted input generally results in no output at all, but these last few weeks, you have put in the time, the effort, the thought and the energy, which deserves to bring incredible results. Not only that, but you understand what drives and motivates you now better than ever before, and you can use that valuable knowledge to excel in your career journey.

Determination and Persistence

When you're working towards your ideal future, you know that not every day will be perfect. You have to be able to keep progressing, even when the easiest thing to do is fall back into your comfort zone. You've already shown remarkable resilience and persistence to get this far. Remember those Power Moves you've been working on – keep them going and they'll help you maintain forward momentum.

Personal Commitment

You've said what you'll do and then you've done what you said. That's commitment. Stick with it.

I'm going to remind you of something I said right at the beginning. This book can help you achieve amazing things for your future, but …

THE ONLY PERSON WHO CAN ACTUALLY MAKE IT HAPPEN IS YOU.

WHERE NEXT?

You've reached the end of the programme and the end of the book – a phenomenal achievement in itself.

As you continue to bring your plan to life and take action to get what you want out of work, this is the start of something very exciting for you.

I can't wait to hear your story as your mindset changes and you journey towards your perfect working life. Tag #theideamindset on social media and you'll be able to connect with other people who are on the same path as you.

You've already started, now your challenge is to maintain momentum.

You've got a profound understanding of yourself, you've got new tools at your disposal to navigate the ups and downs and you've got the team around you to help keep you on track and accountable. It all adds up to your IDEA Mindset – clarity of thought, clarity of decision-making, decisiveness and confidence – a mindset that will result in your dream career. You'll notice that clarity emerging, week by week, month by month. Look back from time to time and notice how things have changed for you. Sometimes you don't see how deep the valley was until you're at the top of the mountain.

'In a dark place we find ourselves, and a little more knowledge lights our way.'

YODA

There will be choices and challenges along the way. New career opportunities will arise which haven't even entered your mind yet. Use the knowledge and tools at your disposal, take control and be confident to intentionally shape the career path ahead of you. As you face new challenges, don't be afraid to ask for help – you're not alone on this voyage.

Enjoy the journey.

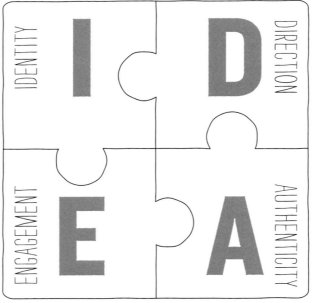

SPACE FOR SCRIBBLES

Here are some blank pages for you to jot down your thoughts, ideas and musings.

....

....

....

....

....

....

....

....

....

....

....

....

....

....

....

....

....

....

....

....

....

RECOMMENDED READING

There is a huge variety of books available which can help you as you continue your journey. Below are some that you may find interesting to explore.

Books About Activating Your Strengths

Now, Discover Your Strengths by Gallup (Gallup Press, 2020)

Strengths Based Leadership: Great Leaders, Teams, and Why People Follow by Gallup (Gallup Press, 2009)

First, Break All the Rules: What the World's Greatest Managers Do Differently by Gallup and Jim Harter (Gallup Press, 2016)

It's the Manager: Moving from Boss to Coach by Jim Clifton and Jim Harter (Gallup Press, 2019)

Wellbeing at Work: How to Build Resilient and Thriving Teams by Jim Clifton and Jim Harter (Gallup Press, 2021)

Books About Taking Control

Feel the Fear and Do It Anyway: How to Turn Your Fear and Indecision into Confidence and Action by Susan Jeffers (Vermilion, 2019)

The Art of Possibility: Transforming Professional and Personal Life by Rosamund Stone Zander and Ben Zander (Harvard Business Review Press, 2000)

Emotional Agility: Get Unstuck, Embrace Change and Thrive in Work and Life by Susan David (Penguin, 2016)

You Do You: How to Be Who You Are and Use What You've Got to Get What You Want by Sarah Knight (Quercus, 2017)

Will It Make the Boat Go Faster? Olympic-winning Strategies for Everyday Success by Ben Hunt-Davis and Harriet Beveridge (Matador, 2011)

The Chimp Paradox: The Mind Management Programme to Help You Achieve Success, Confidence and Happiness by Professor Steve Peters (Vermilion, 2012)

Mindset: Changing the Way You Think to Fulfil Your Potential by Dr Carol S. Dweck (Robinson, 2017)

Books About Designing Your Career

Start With Why: How Great Leaders Inspire Everyone to Take Action by Simon Sinek (Penguin, 2011)

What Got You Here Won't Get You There: How Successful People Become Even More Successful by Marshall Goldsmith (Profile, 2008)

The Squiggly Career: Ditch the Ladder, Discover Opportunity, Design Your Career by Helen Tupper and Sarah Ellis (Portfolio Penguin, 2020)

What Color Is Your Parachute? Your Guide to a Lifetime of Meaningful Work and Career Success by Richard N. Bolles and Katharine Brooks (Berkeley Publishing Corporation, 2020)

How to Get a Job You Love by John Lees (McGraw-Hill Education, 2018)

Lean In: Women, Work, and the Will to Lead by Sheryl Sandberg (Penguin Random House, 2013)

Books About Wellbeing

The Wellbeing Journal: Creative Activities to Inspire, in aid of Mind (Michael O'Mara, 2017)

Think Like a Monk: Train Your Mind for Peace and Purpose Every Day by Jay Shetty (Thorsons, 2020)

The Sleep Revolution: Transforming Your Life, One Night at a Time by Arianna Huffington (Penguin Random House, 2016)

Ikigai: The Japanese Secret to a Long and Happy Life by Héctor Garcia and Francesc Miralles (Hutchinson, 2017)

This Book Could Save Your Life: The Science of Living Longer Better by Graham Lawton with *New Scientist* (John Murray, 2020)

Feel Better in 5: Your Daily Plan to Feel Great for Life by Dr Rangan Chatterjee (Penguin Life, 2019)

The Doctor's Kitchen: Supercharge Your Health with 100 Delicious Everyday Recipes by Dr Rupy Aujla (Thorsons, 2017)

Drink? The New Science of Alcohol and Your Health by Professor David Nutt (Yellow Kite, 2020)

REFERENCES

1. CliftonStrengths Top 5, Gallup.com: https://www.gallup.com/cliftonstrengths

2. 'To unleash people's strengths, help them manage weaknesses', Gallup.com, 3 May 2019: https://www.gallup.com/cliftonstrengths/en/266435/unleash-people-strengths-help-manage-weaknesses.aspx

3. 'New Study Reveals Employees Spend Nearly 1/3 of Time Doing "Pointless" Tasks', Webexpenses.com, 11 June 2019: https://www.webexpenses.com/gb/2019/06/new-study-employees-time-pointless-tasks/

4. Quotes sourced from various published interviews: Williams, Sally, 'Katarina Johnson-Thompson: "I moved to France, split up with my boyfriend, changed my coach ... I changed my life"', *Daily Telegraph*, 31 August 2019: https://www.telegraph.co.uk/womens-sport/0/katarina-johnson-thompson-moved-france-split-boyfriend-changed/; 'Athlete Profile: Katarina Johnson-Thompson', WorldAthletics.org: https://worldathletics.org/athletes/great-britain-ni/katarina-johnson-thompson-14276543; Henson, Mike, 'Katarina Johnson-Thompson: How heptathlete struck gold in Doha', BBC Sport, 30 May 2020: https://www.bbc.co.uk/sport/athletics/52839003; Broadbent, Rick, 'Coach pays for KJT's Rio hell', *The Times*, 23 September 2016: https://www.thetimes.co.uk/article/coach-pays-for-johnson-thompson-rio-hell-jjv58zh3n; John, Emma, 'Katarina Johnson-Thompson: my journey to becoming a world champion', *Financial Times*, 5 December 2019: https://www.ft.com/content/a99a6cc0-1623-11ea-9ee4-11f260415385; Kelner, Martha, 'Katarina Johnson-Thompson was scared to compete or even train ... but a move to France may help turn her into Great Britain's next Golden Girl', *Mail on Sunday*, 13 May 2017: https://www.dailymail.co.uk/sport/othersports/

article-4503326/Katarina-Johnson-Thompson-moved-France.html; 'Katarina Johnson-Thompson "excited" for future after banishing demons at European Championships', *Daily Telegraph*, 11 August 2018: https://www.telegraph.co.uk/athletics/2018/08/11/katarina-johnson-thompson-excited-future-banishing-demons-european/; Bloom, Ben, 'Katarina Johnson-Thompson: "I've not enjoyed anything over the last two years"', *Daily Telegraph*, 12 February 2017: https://www.telegraph.co.uk/athletics/2017/02/12/katarina-johnson-thompson-not-enjoyed-anything-last-two-years/; ——, 'Katarina Johnson-Thompson: "The worst things have happened. Now I'm ready to make new memories"', *Daily Telegraph*, 5 August 2017: https://www.telegraph.co.uk/athletics/2017/08/05/katarina-johnson-thompson-hoping-fulfil-rich-potential-london/; Henson, Mike, 'Katarina Johnson-Thompson on Jodie Comer, sacrifices, and the south of France', BBC Sport, 25 June 2019: https://www.bbc.co.uk/sport/athletics/48647608; McRae, Donald, 'Katarina Johnson-Thompson: "I didn't want to be at the Rio Olympics but I'm ready for Tokyo"', *Guardian*, 13 December 2019: https://www.theguardian.com/sport/2019/dec/13/katarina-johnson-thompson-world-champion-athletics-interview-tokyo-2020; Ingle, Sean, 'Katarina Johnson-Thompson goes to Doha on back of "best run-in ever"', *Guardian*, 21 September 2019: https://www.theguardian.com/sport/2019/sep/21/katarina-johnson-thompson-world-championships-doha-best-prreparation; Chowdhury, Saj, 'Katarina Johnson-Thompson wins World Athletics Championships heptathlon gold', BBC Sport, 3 October 2019: https://www.bbc.co.uk/sport/athletics/49924526; 'Johnson-Thompson caps World Heptathlon title with British Record', British Athletics, 3 October 2019: https://www.britishathletics.org.uk/news-and-features/johnson-thompson-caps-world-heptathlon-title-with-british-record/; 'Exclusive Katarina Johnson-Thompson interview: "Being world champion has an authority to it … but I have the same emotions, doubts and fears"', *Daily Telegraph*, 17 October 2019: https://www.telegraph.co.uk/athletics/2019/10/17/exclusive-katarina-johnson-thompson-interview-world-champion/; Smith, Josh, 'Katarina Johnson-Thompson's powerful words on overcoming an "identity crisis" and learning to love her body are all the inspo you need RN', *Glamour*, 28 February 2020: https://www.glamourmagazine.co.uk/article/katarina-johnson-thompson-tokyo-olympics-2020-interview

5. 'How to get to sleep', NHS: https://www.nhs.uk/live-well/sleep-and-tiredness/how-to-get-to-sleep/

6. 'Why lack of sleep is bad for your health', NHS: 30 May 2018: https://www.nhs.uk/live-well/sleep-and-tiredness/why-lack-of-sleep-is-bad-for-your-health/

7. 'Eat well', NHS, 27 March 2019: https://www.nhs.uk/live-well/eat-well/

8. 'Exercise health benefits', NHS, 11 June 2018: https://www.nhs.uk/live-well/exercise/exercise-health-benefits/

9. 'Exercise guidelines for adults aged 19 to 64', NHS, 8 October 2019: https://www.nhs.uk/live-well/exercise/#guidelines-for-adults-aged-19-to-64

10. 'Exercise after injury', WebMD: https://www.webmd.com/fitness-exercise/exercise-after-injury#2.

11. Kübler-Ross, Elisabeth, *On Death and Dying* (Routledge, 1969)

12. 'Resilience and change', Open University, 2012: https://www.open.edu/openlearn/ocw/mod/oucontent/view.php?id=64961&section=4.

13. Wu, Jade, 'Don't Let Common Thinking Traps Get You Stuck', Psychology Today, 3 March 2020: https://www.psychologytoday.com/gb/blog/the-savvy-psychologist/202003/dont-let-common-thinking-traps-get-you-stuck

Gary Crotaz and Mildred Yuan-Crotaz, WDSF
Professional Division, Salou, Spain, December 2012

ABOUT THE AUTHOR

Dr Gary Crotaz, PhD is something of an expert in career change, having trained as a doctor, worked in science, strategy consulting and senior corporate leadership, and travelled the world as a professional ballroom dancer.

These days he's an executive strengths and mindset coach and has coached clients in more than 15 countries, specialising in activating their unique talents and strengths to achieve ambitious personal and professional goals. *The IDEA Mindset* is his tried-and-tested blueprint for designing your dream career, developed from what Gary learned on his own fascinating journey to career fulfilment.

Gary lives in the UK with his wife, Mildred, and their fluffy dogs Mochi and Beansprout.

www.garycrotaz.com

 @garycrotaz